YOU GOTTA SEE THIS

CINDY PEARLMAN is a syndicated entertainment writer for the New York Times Syndicate and the *Chicago Sun-Times*. She interviews all of the top people in the entertainment industry for her column, "The Big Picture." Her work also appears in several national and international magazines. She is the coauthor of several books, including *The Black Book of Hollywood Beauty Secrets, Simple Things, It's Not About the Horse, Flex Ability, I'm Still Hungry, Love Notes,* and *To Serve with Love.*

YOU GOTTA SEE THIS

More Than 100 of Hollywood's Best

Reveal and Discuss Their Favorite Films

CINDY PEARLMAN

A PLUME BOOK

PLUME
Published by Penguin Group
Penguin Group (USA) Inc., 375 Hudson Street, New York, New York 10014, U.S.A.
Penguin Group (Canada), 90 Eglinton Avenue East, Suite 700,
Toronto, Ontario, Canada M4P 2Y3 (a division of Pearson Penguin Canada Inc.)
Penguin Books Ltd., 80 Strand, London WC2R 0RL, England
Penguin Ireland, 25 St. Stephen's Green, Dublin 2, Ireland (a division of Penguin Books Ltd.)
Penguin Group (Australia), 250 Camberwell Road,
Camberwell, Victoria 3124, Australia (a division of Pearson Australia Group Pty. Ltd.)
Penguin Books India Pvt. Ltd., 11 Community Centre, Panchsheel Park,
New Delhi – 110 017, India
Penguin Books (NZ), cnr Airborne and Rosedale Roads, Albany, Auckland 1310,
New Zealand (a division of Pearson New Zealand Ltd.)
Penguin Books (South Africa) (Pty.) Ltd., 24 Sturdee Avenue, Rosebank,
Johannesburg 2196, South Africa

Penguin Books Ltd., Registered Offices: 80 Strand, London WC2R 0RL, England

First published by Plume, a member of Penguin Group (USA) Inc.

First Printing, February 2007
1 3 5 7 9 10 8 6 4 2

Copyright © Cindy Pearlman, 2007
All rights reserved

 REGISTERED TRADEMARK—MARCA REGISTRADA

LIBRARY OF CONGRESS CATALOGING-IN-PUBLICATION DATA

Pearlman, Cindy, 1964–
You gotta see this : more than 100 of Hollywood's best reveal and
discuss their favorite films / Cindy Pearlman.
p.   cm.
ISBN 978-0-452-28823-2
1. Motion pictures.   2. Motion picture producers and directors—Interviews.   I. Title.
PN1994.P365 2007
791.43'75—dc22   2006019988

Printed in the United States of America
Set in Electra
Designed by Joseph Rutt

BOOKS ARE AVAILABLE AT QUANTITY DISCOUNTS WHEN USED TO PROMOTE PRODUCTS OR SERVICES. FOR
INFORMATION PLEASE WRITE TO PREMIUM MARKETING DIVISION, PENGUIN GROUP (USA) INC., 375 HUDSON
STREET, NEW YORK, NEW YORK 10014.

This book is dedicated to film fans everywhere.
And to one in particular,
Joyce Persico,
one of the great film critics—
and an even better friend.

CONTENTS

Introduction   xi

Joan Allen   1
Tim Allen   3
Robert Altman   4
Anthony Anderson   6
Naveen Andrews   8
Jennifer Aniston   9

Carroll Ballard   11
Antonio Banderas   13
Fenton Bailey and
    Randy Barbato   15
Jack Black   17
Brenda Blethyn   19
Spencer Breslin   21
Adrien Brody   23
James L. Brooks   24
Joy Bryant   25

Jim Carrey   26
Helena Bonham Carter   28
Cedric the Entertainer   30
George Clooney   32
Rob Cohen   34

Chris Columbus   36
Rachael Leigh Cook   38
Dane Cook   39
David Cronenberg   41
Elisha Cuthbert   43

John Dahl   44
Matt Damon   46
Kristin Davis   48
Daniel Day-Lewis   50
Jonathan Demme   53
Johnny Depp   55
Zooey Deschanel   57
Vin Diesel   59
Jerry Douglas   61
Fran Drescher   64
Richard Dreyfuss   66
Minnie Driver   68
David Duchovny   70

Kimberly Elise   72

Peter Farrelly and
    Bobby Farrelly   74
Jon Favreau   77

America Ferrera	79	Jet Li	136
50 Cent	81	Delroy Lindo	138
Naomi Foner	82	Lindsay Lohan	140
James Franco	84	Michael London	142
Morgan Freeman	86	Jennifer Lopez	143
Stephen Gaghan	88	Jena Malone	145
Richard Gere	90	Garry Marshall	146
Terry Gilliam	92	Rob Marshall	148
Akiva Goldsman	94	Jesse L. Martin	150
		Rachel McAdams	152
Alyson Hannigan	96	Paul McGuigan	153
Woody Harrelson	97	Fernando Meirelles	155
Josh Hartnett	99	Neil Meron	156
Salma Hayek	101	Ryan Merriman	158
Dianne Houston	103	Michelle Monaghan	160
Terrence Howard	104	Mo'Nique	162
Kate Hudson	106	Julianne Moore	163
Felicity Huffman	108	Viggo Mortensen	165
		Emily Mortimer	167
Peter Jackson	110		
Tim Johnson	112	Bill Paxton	169
Tommy Lee Jones	114		
		Dennis Quaid	171
Nicole Kidman	116		
Q' Orianka Kilcher	118	Daniel Radcliffe	172
Val Kilmer	119	Harold Ramis	173
Chris Klein	121	Brett Ratner	175
		Jonathan Rhys Meyers	177
Queen Latifah	123	AnnaSophia Robb	179
Sanaa Lathan	125	Brian Robbins	181
Cloris Leachman	127	Robert Rodriguez	183
Heath Ledger	129	Ray Romano	185
John Leguizamo	130	Gena Rowlands	187
Téa Leoni	132	Kurt Russell	188
Eugene Levy	134	Adam Sandler	189

Contents

Peter Sarsgaard 190
Liev Schreiber 192
Joel Schumacher 194
Martin Scorsese 196
Jim Sheridan 199
John Singleton 201
Imelda Staunton 203
Donald Sutherland 204
Tilda Swinton 206
Wanda Sykes 208

Larenz Tate 210
Charlize Theron 212
Uma Thurman 214
Robert Towne 216

Blair Underwood 218

Vince Vaughn 220

Mark Wahlberg 222
Paul Walker 224
Denzel Washington 226
Ken Watanabe 228
Forest Whitaker 229
Bruce Willis 231
Owen Wilson 233
Patrick Wilson 235
Reese Witherspoon 236
Elijah Wood 238
Evan Rachel Wood 239
Alfre Woodard 241

Catherine Zeta-Jones 243

Acknowledgments 245
Index 247

INTRODUCTION

Jodie Foster wouldn't answer the question.

There was no hesitation in her voice. She just absolutely refused by shaking her head and closing those intense blue eyes. "It's like asking which arm I like better or which child I like the best. I just can't even go there."

That's all the screen legend could say on the matter. It was a wrap.

By contrast, Martin Scorsese answered the question in such great detail that seasons seemed to change as he went on and on and on. Director Joel Schumacher got tears in his eyes because the question reminded him of the loss of his father. Jennifer Aniston answered the question and embarrassed an even bigger star who coincidentally drifted into the room. And then there was George Clooney, who turned the question into a cry for action and a comment about a lackadaisical America.

Rapper 50 Cent—now an actor—called off his "boys" in order to answer. "Don't be disrespectin' this girl doin' the askin' because I wanna answer this one. It's important to me." At that point, two 300-pound bodyguards sensed this was serious and backed off. The song stylist, whose real name is Curtis Jackson, spent the next ten minutes in deep thought. "Kids will read this. They'll wanna know," he said.

Bobby Farrelly, half of the wild directing brothers who created *There's Something About Mary*, sort of, kind of, didn't even get the question, but perhaps that was the fault of the interviewer—or maybe it went a little deeper. "This goes to show where my head is. I was going to talk about one of ours," he said. "But this isn't about what I created, but what was created that gave us our chance."

For all of those who love film, the inquiry was easy to ponder but difficult to commit to on a forever basis. (Hell, this was even a tougher commitment than some of these icon's last marriages.)

The question wasn't about their art, their finances, or even their current romantic entanglements.

It was a question regular folk ask their family, friends, and co-workers routinely just to make conversation: *What is your favorite film of all time?*

Over the last two years, the question was posed to Hollywood elite and culled from a series of interviews with the makers and shakers in New York and Los Angeles. Even Harry Potter weighed in by putting his hands on his sixteen-year-old hips, ignoring the throng of screaming girls on the red carpet in London, and saying, "Of course, my favorite movie is *12 Angry Men*. All that angst! All that drama! I just love it!" You could blame puberty. But the good news is at least he didn't pick *Dude, Where's My Car?*

That isn't to say some choices weren't surprising or just downright baffling. On a rainy Saturday afternoon, the always interesting and perplexing Christopher Walken looked even more pensive than normal when the favorite-movie question was posed. "My favorite movie? A . . . movie . . . that . . . is . . . my . . . favorite," he pondered. It might have been easier to ask him to explain Creation.

Still later: Mr. Walken, if it was a rainy Sunday afternoon and you could pop any film you loved into the DVD player, what would it be? *Lightbulb time.*

"Right now, I'd definitely watch a zombie movie," he replied. Not *Citizen Kane*. Not *Gone With the Wind*. A *zombie movie*.

Scant moments later: "Yes, definitely some of my favorite films are zombie movies."

It's still hard to figure out if he was kidding.

Others, well, they picked from the heart as well. They punctuated their choice with the key words: "Oh God, I love that movie."

Can you guess which vixen picked *Kitten with a Whip* or what good old boy from Texas chose a David Lean classic? And what Hobbit has a *Harvey* habit? Just like you can't judge a book by its cover, you can't judge a movie by its lover.

Some films kept cropping up again and again, and certain actors wanted to know if anyone just happened to choose one of their classics. And some of the classics were never even uttered. We're sorry Mr. Hitchcock, but *Vertigo*, a great film by any standards, didn't make this cut. Bette Davis might be a tad upset to know that in current-day Hollywood it's not "All About Eve."

Luckily, the words "The Dukes of Hazzard" never passed the lips of anyone who went on record. We can all be thankful for small favors. But on a quiet Friday afternoon in Hollywood, a major comedic star asked—no, make that begged—"Can't I say *The Wizard of Oz*? I'll say my mom used to make me watch it."

In the end, some of the subjects were a tad prickly, some refused to go on record, and some probably missed their afternoon call on the set because somewhere they're still thinking it over.

Many of the films selected said more about the actors than all of the interviews they could ever dole out to the press and the public. Denzel Washington learned about real street life at the movies while watching *The Education of Sonny Carson* and went on to win an Oscar for being streetwise in *Training Day*. Daniel Day-Lewis has played many tortured Irishmen in his movies and still identifies with the bullied child in *Kes*. Salma Hayek came to the United States from Mexico without knowing more than a handful of words in English. She figures her entire life since then has been about winning the golden ticket. It figures that her favorite film to this day is *Willy Wonka & the Chocolate Factory*.

Boston tough guy Mark Wahlberg almost wanted a verbal retraction after blurting out *Taxi Driver*. He let the choice stand but wouldn't give much of why it was his favorite film. "Well, I think that's gonna give you a little too much insight into my own twisted mind," Wahlberg said with a wicked laugh.

A few Hollywood luminaries might have had the same fear, which is why they refused to see and tell.

Famous director Werner Herzog turned downright belligerent when asked to list his choices. "Do you have time for me to list hundreds of titles?" he asked. Then he scolded, "Your readers should find out and make their own choices." And then he was down on the choices that lurk out there in the dark. "Until I was eleven, I hadn't seen any movies. I didn't know cinema existed. My first film was about the Eskimos building an igloo."

It didn't hurt to go on a fishing expedition. Was it one of his favorites?

"Favorites!" Herzog yelled. "I thought they did a lousy job. I grew up in the snow and the ice and I could tell those Eskimos were doing a very bad job, so it was a bad movie."

It seems that everyone is a critic—or is it a cynic?

As for Jodie, well, others picked her movies as their own choice, including *Taxi Driver*.

"Really? Who said that?" Foster wanted to know. Yes, she was talkin' to me, and hard to refuse. She does have Hannibal Lecter's home phone number.

Jodie will have to wait until pages 23, 173, and 222.

It seems that she can't handle the question, but like everyone else, still wants the answer.

YOU GOTTA SEE THIS

JOAN ALLEN

I have two favorite movies from two different genres. I love *Talk to Her*. My favorite thing about it is this one scene where everything stops and they play this beautiful song on the beach with this couple there. You can literally feel the breeze and the beauty of these Spanish people.

It's just exquisite.

I also love *The Deer Hunter*. There are scenes in that movie that just blow me away. Robert De Niro gives a wonderful performance. It's actually some of the finest acting I've ever seen. It's so complex. He's trying to be the leader and he's furious, terrified, and the acting is on many levels. It's layered. It's powerful, powerful stuff.

TALK TO HER (2002). Winner of a best screenplay Oscar and nominated for best director for colorful Pedro Almodóvar, *Talk to Her* explores the relationships two men have with their comatose girlfriends. The men strike up a friendship while visiting the women, and all four lives cross as destiny intervenes.

THE DEER HUNTER (1978). Michael Cimino won Oscars for best director and best film, along with winners supporting actor Christopher Walken, the film's editor, and sound crew. Fellow nominees Robert De Niro (actor), Meryl Streep (supporting actress), cinematographer, and original screenplay did not. A gritty, realistic drama peppered with raw language, it demonstrated the effect Vietnam had on a trio of Pennsylvania factory workers who were drafted. Walken's game of Russian roulette is one of the most memorable sequences in the film. On a romantic note, Streep and co-star John Cazale were dating during the filming. Cazale is best remembered as the brother Al Pacino orders killed in *The Godfather* saga.

....

Regal, classic beauty **JOAN ALLEN** hails from Rochelle, Illinois, where she got her start in acting by performing with the now legendary Steppenwolf Theatre Company. In addition to stage work, Allen has starred in the movies *Manhunter*, *Peggy Sue Got Married*, *Tucker: The Man and His Dreams*, *In Country*, *Searching for Bobby Fischer*, *Nixon*, *The Crucible*, *The Ice Storm*, *Pleasantville*, *The Notebook*, *The Bourne Supremacy*, *Yes*, and *The Upside of Anger*.

TIM ALLEN

Oh, this is so easy because it's *The Seven Samurai*. There are so many great themes combined with really stirring dialogue. I know you're thinking I should say a comedy, but when I go to see a movie I like to see something deeper. I love a film that's a great tragedy, and there is no greater tragedy than *Seven Samurai*. It's a job so well done that Hollywood could never re-create it. There will never be a remake and that's the ultimate compliment. And I should know. I've done a re-make! All I can tell you is that this film holds up for me even though when I see it now it looks so old. But it still grabs me every single time. Even with the subtitles. And I'm not a guy for subtitles.

THE SEVEN SAMURAI (1954). Japanese filmmaker Akira Kurosawa's acclaimed masterwork, this is a much-imitated but rarely equaled drama about a village that hires samurai to help fend off marauding bandits. In return for food, the warriors teach the villagers how to fight back. Toshirô Mifune emerged from the film a major star while its costume and art direction received Oscar nominations.

Funny man **TIM ALLEN** started out as a stand-up comedian who rose to fame on the hit TV series *Home Improvement*. He has starred in a slew of number one movies, including *Toy Story* and *Toy Story 2*, *The Santa Clause* and *The Santa Clause 2*, *Joe Somebody*, *Christmas with the Kranks*, and *The Shaggy Dog*.

ROBERT ALTMAN

I love *Brief Encounter*. I was nineteen or twenty when I saw it for the first time. What I got out of it was that older women who wear sensible shoes are also attractive. Very attractive. The film had a big impression on me. I also love *Persona*. I love the personalities in it and I've emulated them in a few films.

BRIEF ENCOUNTER (1945). Celia Johnson and Trevor Howard star in the romantic tale of a woman and a man who are total strangers, but a chance encounter at a railway station changes everything for them. Both are already married, but fall deeply in love, which leads to regular Thursday meetings at a café where they're tempted by what is forbidden.

PERSONA (1966). Written and directed by Ingmar Bergman, the film revolves around a nurse played by Bibi Andersson, who must tend to an actress named Elisabeth Vogler played by Liv Ullmann. The actress can't speak, but somehow the two women find their own distinct personas are melding together.

....

Kansas city native **ROBERT ALTMAN** is one of the most distinctive film directors of all time. He has helmed classics including *M*∗*A*∗*S*∗*H*; *McCabe & Mrs. Miller*; *California Split*; *Nashville*; *3 Women*; *Come Back to the Five and Dime, Jimmy Dean, Jimmy Dean*; *The Player*; *Short Cuts*; *Kansas City*; and *Dr. T and the Women*. Well into his senior years, he refuses to retire and recently called the shots for the ensemble films *Gosford Park* and *A Prairie Home Companion*, starring Meryl Streep and Kevin Kline.

ANTHONY ANDERSON

Off the top of my head, I'll give you a fast three favorites. Those are *Fast Times at Ridgemont High, Lean on Me,* and *Cooley High.* I love school movies. I don't know why.

But this need to go back to school is really only part of it. More than anything else, I love to watch actors transform themselves. Let's take *Ridgemont High.* I look at Sean Penn and what he did with that character of Jeff Spicoli and I know I'll never forget that character. Then I look at Sean's career now and where he is, and realize that this wasn't some high school movie. This was a great actor creating a brilliant character.

I'm also a huge fan of *Good Morning, Vietnam* and *The Dead Poets Society.* I love what Robin Williams did with both of those characters. Robin was known as a comedian, and he obviously wanted to make a change. These are the two movies that took him to the other side. I love watching actors on the brink of that type of change, and I look at the performances they gave in those breakthrough movies instead of just at the movies.

Do I have to stop now? Because really I could go on and on. I love Tom Hanks in *Splash.* The guy was on *Bosom Buddies* and then suddenly he's starring in a great movie with Daryl Hannah. Jamie Foxx was on *In Living Color* and then suddenly he gave one of my favorite performances of all time in *Ray.* I love to watch transitions. These comics really went to the dramatic side and made it all the way. But any comedian knows that you can do it. Our laughter comes from pain and our willingness to be vulnerable.

....

FAST TIMES AT RIDGEMONT HIGH (1982). Director Amy Heckerling complained about the editing of her coming-of-age teen comedy-drama, but its good humor and hard truths have withstood the test of time. Jennifer Jason Leigh plays the virgin who's all too eager to lose her virginity to a jerk. But it's Sean Penn's indelible comic performance as laid-back stoner-surfer Jeff Spicoli whose scenes with exasperated teacher Ray Walston steal the most attention in Cameron Crowe's script. The movie is now part of the National Film Registry.

LEAN ON ME (1989). Real-life Paterson, New Jersey, principal Joe Clark carried a baseball bat through the halls of the rough inner-city school he turned around with his no-nonsense approach. In John G. Avildsen's inspirational screen version, Morgan Freeman played Clark and filmed his scenes in the actual school Clark headed.

COOLEY HIGH (1975). Director Michael Schultz is best known for his work on *Car Wash*, but in this more serious film, two urban Chicago high school buddies cross paths with criminals and end up falsely accused of stealing a car. Starring Glynn Turman and Lawrence Hilton-Jacobs, the film chronicles what happens at the end of a school year.

....

Tough guy **ANTHONY ANDERSON** recently starred for Martin Scorsese in *The Departed*. Prior films include *Life*; *Liberty Heights*; *Big Momma's House*; *Me, Myself & Irene*; *Kingdom Come*; *Exit Wounds*; *Two Can Play That Game*; *Barbershop*; *Malibu's Most Wanted*; *Hustle & Flow*; *Scary Movie 3* and *4*; and *The Last Stand*. He also plays gang leader Antwon Mitchell on the hit FX series *The Shield*.

NAVEEN ANDREWS

I was brought up as a Christian, so I'm going to mention a film of faith, which is *The Last Temptation of Christ* by Martin Scorsese. It's a film by a true believer. Mr. Scorsese takes a subject that isn't easy and makes it understandable to a modern audience.

It's difficult to read the Gospels. But Scorsese achieved clarity on screen with them.

This is also a tremendously moving film. When Christ dies on the cross with what he accomplished in his life I wanted to cheer. It's like, "Good on you, Christ!"

It's also a movie about being human. It asks, What is it to be human? What do we believe? I also like the message of the movie, which to me is that we have divine in all of us.

THE LAST TEMPTATION OF CHRIST (1988). Martin Scorsese raised a thunderstorm of controversy with his depiction of the relationship between Jesus (Willem Dafoe) and Mary Magdalene (Barbara Hershey) in this graphically violent depiction of Christ's final days. Scorsese was nominated for a best director Oscar but did not win.

London native **NAVEEN ANDREWS** played Kip in the Oscar-winning movie *The English Patient*. He also starred in *Kama Sutra: A Tale of Love, True Love and Chaos, Bombay Boys, Mighty Joe Young, Rollerball, Easy,* and *Bride & Prejudice.* He plays Sayid Jarrah in the hit TV series *Lost.*

JENNIFER ANISTON

I've seen *Terms of Endearment* hundreds of times. It's one of those movies where you can turn it on or catch it at any point, and it just makes me burst into tears. It's almost Pavlovian for me. If I turn it on at the point where Shirley MacLaine is demanding her daughter gets her evening medicine in the hospital, I'm weeping with tears running down my cheeks. If it's a later point where Debra Winger is saying good-bye to her children, then I'm a puddle on the floor.

Of course, I can only wish to click the remote late at night and find the part of *Terms* where Shirley is on her first date with Jack Nicholson. She has on that fabulous pink scarf, and you can see on Aurora's face that she really wants to sleep with Garrett, but she's also afraid. What more do you want in a movie but humor, laughter, heartwrenching moments, acting that's superb, and writing that's sublime? It's a fantastic piece of work.

TERMS OF ENDEARMENT (1983). Call her the mother from hell or one hell of a mother, Shirley MacLaine gets both titles as a woman who checks to make sure her daughter is breathing as a little girl and then holds her own breath while her adult daughter marries a man destined to ruin her life. The film won five Academy Awards, including best picture, best director for James L. Brooks, best screenplay for Brooks, best actor for Jack Nicholson, and best actress for Shirley MacLaine, who beat out her co-star, Debra Winger, for the Oscar statue. Everyone knows the film revolves around obsessive mother Aurora Greenway (MacLaine) who clashes over the decades with her long-suffering daughter Emma (Winger). The supporting cast includes Nicholson as the ready-for-lift-off former astronaut, plus Danny DeVito, Jeff Daniels, and John Lithgow. Has anything ever been more heartbreaking than Aurora screaming at those nurses, "Just give my daughter the shot!"

••••••••••••••••••••••••••••••••

New York native **JENNIFER ANISTON** is on the A list of Hollywood's leading ladies. After ten years as television's favorite "Friend" Rachel Green, she has embarked on a screen career that includes *The Good Girl*, *Along Came Polly*, *Rumor Has It*, *The Break-Up*, and *Friends with Money*. She would truly like to forget that she starred in 1993's *Leprechaun*, so please don't bring it up if you see her.

CARROLL BALLARD

God, it's such a hard question. But I do love *The Bad Sleep Well* from Akira Kurosawa. It has the greatest opening scene of any movie in history. This opening just sucks you in. For me that is the mark of really great storytelling. If you have people on the edge of their seats just moments after the lights dim, then you really know what you're doing.

The Bad Sleep Well begins in this big hotel somewhere. There are all these reporters, and they're all waiting for this big event to happen. They're all milling around in the lobby, and then big limos start pulling up. Here comes this mass of people. There's an old guy and this very young girl who is all dressed up in this wedding costume.

This whole procession of reporters follows the guy. It's obviously a big event, and they all walk into this hall where they will have the ceremony. There is a big feast ready. Everyone is sitting there.

The camera goes down the hallway to where the kitchen is, and the doors to the kitchen open up. Here comes this guy pushing this trolley, and on the trolley is this cake in the shape of an office building. The waiter pushes the cake into the hallway down into the room where everyone is sitting.

It comes to rest in front of this old guy. You see the look on this man's face. He's horrified; you don't know what it is. There is a rose hanging out of one of the windows on the cake. This guy completely goes ballistic, then you don't know.

The whole story is that this young guy is marrying the daughter of the head of a major corporation so he can get into the family. That window on the cake is the window his father supposedly jumped out of and killed himself, but he was actually murdered.

And that's just the lead-in. It's all so fantastic. Then you discover where all this comes from . . . and it's so fantastic.

I love that anything that good like that from the beginning is probably going to be great. The entire movie is just very moving, real, and true. It's just really great storytelling.

······································

THE BAD SLEEP WELL (1960). Japanese master Akira Kurosawa directed this Hamlet-like drama of a young man with plans to expose the men responsible for his father's death in postwar Japan. Toshirô Mifune stars in the drama designed to show corruption in corporate Japan.

······································

Director **CARROLL BALLARD** was a UCLA classmate of Francis Ford Coppola, who became the executive producer of their classic film *The Black Stallion*. Ballard has also directed *Never Cry Wolf, Nutcracker: The Motion Picture, Wind, Fly Away Home, The Cruelest Winter*, and *Duma*.

ANTONIO BANDERAS

I love so many movies that we might be here for an entire year. This is truly such a difficult one . . . but if I have to commit, then let me mention one of my favorite filmmakers—Orson Welles. I love everything he did, but two of his movies stand above the rest for me—*Touch of Evil* and *The Magnificent Ambersons*.

The Magnificent Ambersons is one of those movies you rediscover again and again in your life. You forget about it for a minute, but then see it again and realize that it's brilliant. I love the invention of these characters, but even more, I can't believe that Welles did these movies with the beautiful esthetics he put on the screen. I remember one shot from this movie is done in Chinese shadows with five guys in those shadows. Unbelievable.

I love *Touch of Evil* for a simple reason: It's a movie with no morals. Perfect in its creation and theme.

It's all about this filmmaker for me. I find him tremendously inspiring. It doesn't hurt that Orson Welles is buried in a well in my father's village in Spain. His ashes are buried in an old well covered by flowers in Málaga, Spain. The kinship with him just continues.

TOUCH OF EVIL (1958). In a bit of offbeat casting, all-American Charlton Heston played Mexican narcotics official Ramon Miguel "Mike" Vargas in this Orson Welles potboiler about police corruption in a border town. Janet Leigh is cast as Vargas's bride, an innocent caught in the frame-up engineered by a crooked police captain (Welles in bad makeup) who Vargas catches planting evidence in a car-bombing case. The black-and-white thriller has a notable sleaze factor—Akim Tamiroff watching Leigh squirm on a bed—and is populated by bizarre characters, like the nervous motel clerk played by Dennis Weaver. Even Marlene Dietrich figures into this one.

THE MAGNIFICENT AMBERSONS (1942). Orson Welles was still a wunderkind when he directed this Oscar-nominated drama about a doomed romance that receives a second chance only to be sabotaged by a jealous son and his aunt (Agnes Moorehead). Joseph Cotten and Anne Baxter played the star-crossed lovers, and Tim Holt the intruding son in a film nominated for best picture, cinematography, art direction, and supporting actress (Moorehead).

....

Handsome superstar **ANTONIO BANDERAS** hails from Málaga, Spain, where he began his acting career working in a small Spanish theater company and then as an ensemble member of the prestigious National Theater of Spain. In 1982 Banderas was cast by writer-director Pedro Almodóvar in *Labyrinth of Passion*, and it became the first of five films he would do with Almodóvar, including *Matador, Law of Desire, Women on the Verge of a Nervous Breakdown,* and *Tie Me Up! Tie Me Down!* His American films include *The Mambo Kings, Once Upon a Time in Mexico, Spy Kids, Assassins, Philadelphia, Evita,* and *The Legend of Zorro.* He also voices the popular character of Puss in Boots in the animated blockbusters *Shrek 2* and *Shrek the Third.* He directed *Crazy in Alabama* and the Spanish film *El Camino de los ingleses.*

FENTON BAILEY AND RANDY BARBATO

FENTON BAILEY:

I have a soft spot for sci-fi, and my favorite film is a metaphor for the times we live in. At first glance it's a take on the Holocaust, but some of the ideas explored in it are relevant to today and how we define and conceive our enemies. This is our potential undoing.

The movie I'm talking about is *Starship Troopers*. Technically, it's a fun movie about a bunch of kids killing these giant metal spiders. That makes it fun, but it's so much deeper. I love the whole idea that there is this race of bugs that we have treated like scum, yet the bugs display incredible intelligence and sensitivity. We always judge the people we don't know. That's the message of the movie. The film also says that it's so easy to incite hatred, and the results of doing that are cataclysmic.

It's not just a sci-fi flick. This is a very dark and profound film, but because it's so slick and Hollywood glossy, I think people haven't paid attention to it. Everyone should rent it and give it a chance.

RANDY BARBATO:

Oh, my favorite film would have to be *The Sound of Music*. It's got everything—love, music, and action. It's got Julie. It's got the Baroness, or in other words, a drag queen. It's also got all those cute kids. Think about it. *The Sound of Music* is very *American Idol* without Simon

Cowell. Those poor kids are standing on that stage! The only thing that's missing is Paula Abdul. If Simon was in the film, he'd be one of the Nazis. Of course, you also have the beautiful scenery and the costumes.

My grandmother made us watch that film every single summer. Every time, I was terrified during the graveyard scene. Run, Julie, run!

．．．．．．．．．．．．．．．．．．．．．．．．．．．．．．．．

STARSHIP TROOPERS (1997). Huge bugs battled Casper Van Dien in Paul Verhoeven's futuristic adventure in which high school kids are encouraged to join the military. They fight bugs to keep humanity safe. Believe it or not, the over-the-top feature was nominated for best special effects.

THE SOUND OF MUSIC (1965). Even Will and Grace were obsessed with this Julie Andrews classic based on the real-life experiences of the Von Trapp family. Awarded the Oscar for best picture, director (Robert Wise), music, sound, and editing, it told the story of Maria, a woman sent to the home of a retired and widowed naval captain (Christopher Plummer) to care for his brood of seven. Andrews was nominated for best actress, and co-star Peggy Wood competed for best supporting actress. The film received additional nominations for art direction, costuming, and cinematography.

．．．．．．．．．．．．．．．．．．．．．．．．．．．．．．．．

FENTON BAILEY and **RANDY BARBATO** directed the documentary *Inside Deep Throat*, which traced the history of the X-rated cult hit. Both have produced a slew of other documentaries and TV series.

JACK BLACK

I always really loved *One Flew Over the Cuckoo's Nest*. Jack was just so darn good, plus the movie is moving. I guess I love this one so much because I've always had an obsession with people who are psychologically challenged. Wait . . . that doesn't sound good the way it just came out. But I do love people who don't think in the so-called normal way.

I'll take psychological problems any day in a movie over a car chase or a love story. I love to watch people who think way outside the box and in *Cuckoo's Nest*, it's almost like they're in a zoo.

ONE FLEW OVER THE CUCKOO'S NEST (1975). Jack Nicholson assured his place in movie history with his iconoclastic portrait of Randle Patrick McMurphy, a man who convinces prison guards he's nuts enough to require psychiatric care. He gets his wish only to fall into the hands of the very by-the-books Nurse Ratched (Louise Fletcher), who has ways of dealing with unruly patients. Nicholson took home a best actor Oscar for the best film of the year, with more statuettes going to director Milos Forman, lead actress Fletcher, and the screenwriters. Oscar losses included cinematography, music, editing, and supporting actor Brad Dourif.

....

The man known as **JACK BLACK** grew up Santa Monica, California. At UCLA, he joined Tim Robbins's acting group and made his film debut in *Bob Roberts*. He also appeared in *High Fidelity*, *The Cable Guy*, *Mars Attacks!*, *Saving Silverman*, *Shallow Hal*, *Orange County*, *Anchorman: The Legend of Ron Burgundy*, *Nacho Libre*, and *The Holiday*. He played teacher extraordinaire Dewey Finn in the hit *The School of Rock* and Carl Denham in Peter Jackson's remake of *King Kong*. He's half of the rock act Tenacious D.

BRENDA BLETHYN

I love *Calamity Jane* with Doris Day. I think we should sing, *"Oh, the Deadwood stage is a-rollin' on over the plains"* . . . [Ms. Blethyn proceeds to sing the entire song!]

I'm sorry. I'm sorry. It was just so thrilling. There were long shots of Doris Day singing, gunslinging, and sliding along the bar.

I went to the picture when I was twelve. In those days you could go in any old time in England and stay. The program was continuous. I remember going to see *Calamity Jane* for the first time in the wee morning and stayed past ten at night until there was a torch shone in my face. At the other end of the torch was a policeman and my mum was standing next to him. Ooooh, I thought I was in big trouble. Everyone thought I was missing, but I was spending the day with Doris.

CALAMITY JANE (1953). Doris Day plays the title role of a tough Indian scout who romanced Wild Bill Hickok (Howard Keel) and could hit all the right notes at the same time. The lively musical won an Oscar for its song *Secret Love*, and was nominated for best score and sound.

••••••••••••••••••••••••••••••••

A native of Kent, England, and the youngest of nine children, **BRENDA BLETHYN** spent twenty years on stage before breaking into films. Her credits include A *River Runs Through It, The Witches,* and *Secrets & Lies,* which won her a BAFTA Award and an Academy Award nomination. She received a second Oscar nomination for *Little Voice.* She recently played Mrs. Bennet in *Pride & Prejudice.* She would love to do a musical. "Everything to me is a cue for a song," she muses. "Inside my head is a musical."

SPENCER BRESLIN

I really like *2001: A Space Odyssey*. I have to admit that I didn't get this movie at all when I first saw it, because I was only a kid. But then I watched it again. In fact, I popped it in this past year and now I know it's the coolest movie ever.

Why? I could explain it to you, but you really need to figure this movie out for yourself. If I have to put it into words, well, the movie teaches you about evolution. Plus, it's sci-fi. Yeah, it's all kind of confusing, but that's cool in a way, too, because you really need to think about this one. And how many movies make you think anymore?

It's weird that when I watch this movie I get it, but later I can't explain it. I guess that's the way Kubrick wanted the movie to be for people. The deal is you're supposed to figure out the end for yourself. If I had to give the whole thing a theme it's about the savagery of man. Kubrick talks about that in a lot of his movies, including *Dr. Strangelove*, which is cool. But to be honest, I really need to see the rest of his movies. And just seeing *2001* makes me want to see all of his movies. What more can a director do than make you want to see all of his films?

2001: A SPACE ODYSSEY (1968). A talking computer named HAL was way ahead of his time in Stanley Kubrick's futuristic adventure as an astronaut and four others head to Jupiter to find the source of a monolith discovered on the moon. HAL starts acting up and the astronaut has to override it and see where curiosity and human intelligence will take him. Although the Kubrick–Arthur C. Clarke screenplay is subject to wide interpretation, the film is considered a classic.

It won nominations for Kubrick, the screenplay, and its art direction, but took home an Oscar only for its influential visual effects.

·····································

Young actor **SPENCER BRESLIN** hails from New York City. He has starred in such films as *The Kid, Meet the Parents, The Santa Clause 2, The Cat in the Hat, Raising Helen, The Princess Diaries 2: Royal Engagement, The Shaggy Dog, Zoom,* and *The Santa Clause 3.* Even when he's busy on a set, he still finds time to do his math homework.

ADRIEN BRODY

When I was a younger man, it was all about the Robert De Niro and Al Pacino movies for me. Couldn't get enough. But if I had to pick just one film that is pretty impressive it's *Taxi Driver*. I've seen it about a zillion times. I love that De Niro plays Travis Bickle as the ultimate lonely guy. Think about it for a minute: There's a little bit of that man in each of us. All of us wish we could free ourselves from those feelings. The movie is amazing because it just breathes the truth, yet it's also very visual, very stylized, and has a lot of subtlety and honesty. The characters are tragic, I guess. Tragedy is fascinating to me. I find this film is a way to process tragedy in my own life. This movie is what still attracts me to characters that exist in their own lonely worlds.

TAXI DRIVER (1976). Shocking for its time, Martin Scorsese's drama about a crazed New York cabbie (Robert De Niro) infatuated with a political worker (Cybill Shepherd) and a child prostitute (Jodie Foster) won no Oscars despite nominations for best picture, lead actor (De Niro), supporting actress (Foster), and music (Bernard Herrmann).

Oscar-winning actor and spontaneous kisser **ADRIEN BRODY** locked lips with a shocked Halle Berry in his excitement over winning an Oscar for playing Warsaw ghetto survivor Wladyslaw Szpilman in Roman Polanski's 2002 film *The Pianist*. The New York native also starred in *The Thin Red Line, Liberty Heights, Summer of Sam, The Village, The Jacket*, and *King Kong*.

JAMES L. BROOKS

My choice might seem odd, but it's *All That Jazz*. In terms of an absolutely original film, it's the best. It's unlike any film that was ever made. Roy Scheider's convincing you that he was a gifted dancer—come on!

ALL THAT JAZZ (1979). The life and times of choreographer Bob Fosse are featured in the film he directed, choreographed, and co-authored. It's not a pretty picture he paints of the self-destructive womanizer portrayed by Roy Scheider. The women in his life—and there are many—are played by Jessica Lange, Ann Reinking (re-creating her own life), and Leland Palmer. The dancing is electric, and the film picked up Oscars for its art direction, costuming, editing, and music. It failed to score in the lead actor (Scheider), cinematography, director, screenplay, and picture categories.

JAMES L. BROOKS is an acclaimed actor, writer, and producer who has directed some of the most meaningful films of our time. He helmed *Terms of Endearment*, *Broadcast News*, *I'll Do Anything*, *As Good As It Gets*, and *Spanglish*. Brooks also directed nine actors in their Oscar-nominated performances: Shirley MacLaine, Jack Nicholson, Debra Winger, John Lithgow, Holly Hunter, William Hurt, Albert Brooks, Helen Hunt, and Greg Kinnear. Of that group, Nicholson, MacLaine, and Hunt won Oscars. He was the executive producer of *The Mary Tyler Moore Show*, *Rhoda*, *Lou Grant*, and *Taxi*. He also developed the legendary TV series *The Simpsons*.

JOY BRYANT

I love Wes Anderson's *Royal Tenenbaums*. He sets up a life unlike any other I've seen on camera. It's real, but it's not. The characters—no matter how little or big—are all subtle. It's all so cool, kooky, and original. You can't compare it to any other movies.

I like that movie from beginning to end. I love when Danny Glover falls. That's pretty funny and brilliant. I also think it's one of Gwyneth's greatest roles ever. She's so dark. And her coat is amazing. I was thinking of making one like that for myself.

THE ROYAL TENENBAUMS (2001). Gene Hackman plays the eccentric father who returns to his family of geniuses after a twenty-year absence to make amends. Directed by Wes Anderson and co-written with Owen Wilson, who is in the cast, the film showcases each of the odd family members. Ben Stiller is the real estate genius with an obsessive character; Gwyneth Paltrow is the depressed playwright; Luke Wilson is a lonely tennis pro; and mother Anjelica Huston isn't sure what to make of her husband's return. Owen Wilson and Anderson shared an Oscar nomination for their original screenplay.

Up-and-coming screen beauty, **JOY BRYANT** is a Bronx native who studied at Yale University. She was a model for Tommy Hilfiger before getting her acting break from director Denzel Washington in *Antwone Fisher*. Bryant has also done roles in *Honey*, *Spider-Man 2*, *Haven*, *The Skeleton Key*, *London*, *Get Rich or Die Tryin'*, and *Bobby*.

JIM CARREY

My favorite movie of all time is *Network*. I like the character of Paddy Chayefsky. It's like a prophecy of what happened in the last fifty years. Every actor scores immensely. It's phenomenal.

Every actor in *Network* has an arc that you want to follow, and there were just themes that were touched upon in the movie that were just so incredibly deep to me. It was illuminating. It was like when . . . I'm sorry, I've forgotten the actor's name . . . wait, it was William Holden . . . okay, when he's in the kitchen talking to his girl-friend, who he has left his wife for, and she's going all over the place about success and how everything is working out great and all of that stuff, and he's trying to get her attention he says, "You're dealing with a man for whom mortality is a real thing, for whom death is a real thing with definable features."

Lines like that make you just go, *Ah, God. Let me say a line like that someday.* That so touches people on a real level.

NETWORK (1976). Now, it all seems like an eerie prediction of the future for the film that won four Oscars, including best actor for Peter Finch, best actress for Faye Dunaway, best supporting actress for Beatrice Straight, and best screenplay for Paddy Chayefsky. The classic revolves around a TV network that exploits an ex-anchor's rants about the media for all-important ratings. Finch's Oscar was awarded posthumously.

．．．．．．．．．．．．．．．．．．．．．．．．．．．．．．

Toronto native **JIM CARREY** knew he was funny as a boy because at age ten, he mailed his résumé to *The Carol Burnett Show*. He was also allowed the last ten minutes of each school day "to do his stand-up routine." Carrey's big break was a role on the TV series *In Living Color*. He broke into films with the box office smash *Ace Ventura: Pet Detective*. His comedic films include *The Mask*, *Dumb & Dumber*, *The Cable Guy*, and *Liar Liar*, and he played the Riddler in *Batman Forever*. Carrey has also taken critically acclaimed dramatic turns in movies, including *Man on the Moon*, where he portrayed Andy Kaufman, *Eternal Sunshine of the Spotless Mind*, *The Truman Show*, and *The Majestic*.

HELENA BONHAM CARTER

Well, I can tell you that Tim [Burton] loves all the Ray Harryhausen films. He also watches *The Exorcist* over and over again. Of course, I have completely different tastes. I love to watch children's movies, and my favorite film of all time is *Mary Poppins*. I love musicals and I love Julie Andrews. I also adore the penguins and all the little animals. It's just such a heartwarming movie. I even modeled a bit of my house on that movie.

I like the captain, too, because he's just such a joy. Can I say one more thing about Julie? She's so beautiful. But more than anything, I love the magic in that movie. I adore the rooftop chimney and the fantastic old England stuff.

MARY POPPINS (1964). Julie Andrews plays the nanny who works her magic on the unhappy family of a banker. The musical star won a best actress Oscar for her work, and the film scored statuettes for visual effects, editing, the original song "Chim Chim Cher-ee," and musical score. It lost in the categories of best picture, art direction, cinematography, costume design, director (Robert Stevenson), score, sound, and adapted screenplay.

....

The multifaceted **HELENA BONHAM CARTER** grew up in London, where she was discovered by the team of Merchant-Ivory who cast her in *A Room with a View* and then *Howards End*. She has also starred in big-screen adaptations of *Hamlet* and *Frankenstein* plus had roles in *Mighty Aphrodite* for Woody Allen and *Fight Club* for director David Fincher. She met mate, director Tim Burton, when he cast her in his remake of *Planet of the Apes*, and together they have a son named Billy Ray. Carter also starred for him in *Big Fish* and *Charlie and the Chocolate Factory*.

CEDRIC THE ENTERTAINER

I got a couple of movies that qualify as favorites. One that my wife and I really love is really silly and called *A Low Down Dirty Shame*. We love that movie. It cracks me up for whatever reason. It's got action. It's just the attitude. I love Jada when she wants to fight. She's like, "Do ya' want some of this?" She's such a little thing.

I love Charles Dutton as this wannabe tough, bad FBI agent. He's screaming, "I'll name names!" He's really, really tough until somebody puts a knife up to him, and he backs right down.

I also love *Scarface*. I like the beginning and the way he shot it. You saw the actual footage of the Cubans coming and living under the freeways. And then you go inside the culture and see that culture of people who left this country where they were being oppressed. They're gonna make it to America any way they can. Al Pacino was really great at playing that main role. I could watch it everytime it's on.

A LOW DOWN DIRTY SHAME (1994). *In Living Color*'s Keenan Ivory Wayans wrote and directed this unpretentious action-comedy about a detective looking for some missing drug money. Jada Pinkett Smith co-starred.

SCARFACE (1983). Brian De Palma directed this Oliver Stone–written Mob classic starring Al Pacino as the infamous Tony Montana. Set in Miami in the 1980s, the film focuses on Cuban immigrant Montana, who runs a drug mecca and lives by his "Greed Is Good" motto. A newcomer named Michelle Pfeiffer played Pacino's main squeeze, Elvira Hancock.

....

CEDRIC THE ENTERTAINER was working as a State Farm Insurance salesman in Missouri when he faced a life's crossroads—secure job or stand-up comedian. He chose the latter. It paid off, because he became one of the Original Kings of Comedy, along with Bernie Mac, Steve Harvey, and D. L. Hughley. His films include *Ride*, *Big Momma's House*, *Kingdom Come*, *Dr. Dolittle 2*, *Ice Age*, *Barbershop*, *Intolerable Cruelty*, *Barbershop 2: Back in Business*, *Johnson Family Vacation*, *Lemony Snicket's A Series of Unfortunate Events*, *Man of the House*, *Be Cool*, and *Madagascar*. He played a new Ralph Kramden in a film version of *The Honeymooners*.

GEORGE CLOONEY

It's a tough one. It's a dual pick for me. It's two that go hand-in-hand, because they're both from the same book.

My favorite films are *Dr. Strangelove* and *Fail-Safe*. They're just brilliant films that say a lot about the world. They talk about issues of nuclear proliferation. They're also so brilliantly made. Lumet made one and Kubrick made the other. One is hysterically funny and the other is terrifying. They're just beautifully made films. Wait, I already said that, but write it down again, please.

Both films are pro-American. They tell me that the whole idea of America is based on dissent and raising questions. That's why we left King George over in England. We wanted to speak out. These movies remind us that we need to always speak out. They say that it's not just your right, but your duty to ask questions.

Can I add *Harold and Maude*, too? Come on! Three films as my favorites aren't too long of a list. I think it's a beautiful story about feelings.

....

DR. STRANGELOVE OR: HOW I LEARNED TO STOP WORRYING AND LOVE THE BOMB (1964). Considered one of Stanley Kubrick's masterworks, this Cold War black comedy stars Peter Sellers as three men attempting to avert a nuclear disaster engineered by a mad U.S. Air Force colonel (Sterling Hayden). It's Sellers who plays an Adlai Stevenson–type U.S. president, a British captain, and the ex-Nazi Strangelove. It's a potent intellectual jab at the absurdity of war and the men who make it, earning Sellers, Kubrick, the film, and its screenplay Oscar nominations.

FAIL-SAFE (1964). Still timely enough for George Clooney to have filmed a recent television version, this stark Sidney Lumet drama puts a U.S. president (Henry Fonda) in the position of allowing Russia to annihilate New York City in return for an accidental U.S. nuclear attack on Moscow. An all-star cast helped carry the import of this edge-of-your-seat drama with a sobering ending.

....

GEORGE CLOONEY is a former *People* magazine "Sexiest Man Alive" and the son of Kentucky TV show host Nick Clooney. George began his career on his father's shows and then became more serious about acting when his cousin Miguel Ferrer helped him land a role in the film classic *Return of the Killer Tomatoes!* Clooney starred on such TV shows as *Roseanne* and *The Facts of Life* before becoming internationally famous as Dr. Doug Ross on the hit series *ER.* At the same time, his film career took off with roles in *From Dusk Till Dawn, One Fine Day, Batman & Robin, The Peacemaker, Out of Sight, Three Kings,* and a TV remake of *Fail-Safe.* He has also starred in *O Brother, Where Art Thou?; The Perfect Storm; Ocean's Eleven;* and *Solaris;* and he directed *Confessions of a Dangerous Mind.* Clooney also directed the critically acclaimed *Good Night, and Good Luck.* He won a best supporting actor Oscar for his role of Bob Barnes in *Syriana.* He also placed all the phone calls to jump-start the sequel *Ocean's Thirteen.*

ROB COHEN

I'm sure you've heard this answer before, but it's *Lawrence of Arabia*. Let me tell you why. I'm into film as giving you the definitive and authentic version of a story. David Lean managed to balance the authentic canvas of the enormity and restaged the Arab revolt.

He put a fascinating character right up front. He also had a script that managed to delineate the political situation from all its levels and duplicities. At the same time, it was a huge action movie.

The spectacle and the intimacy have never been duplicated.

So every time I'm about to make a movie, the last thing I do on a Sunday before the shoot is pop in my copy of *Lawrence of Arabia*. I look up on the screen and go, *These are the aspirations. These are the goals.* You'll never hit it. But you aspire to it, and it reminds you of why I want to be a movie director. Spectacle and intense character are what I've been trying to do in my films as a humble accolade of a man who made that happen.

LAWRENCE OF ARABIA (1962). Playing the enigmatic T. E. Lawrence made Peter O'Toole an international star in David Lean's handsome, Oscar-winning epic depiction of Lawrence's desert adventures with an Arab leader. The film took home Oscars for best film, director (Lean), music (Maurice Jarre), art direction, cinematography, sound, and film editing, but lost in the categories of best actor (O'Toole), supporting actor (Omar Sharif), and adapted screenplay.

New York native and Harvard graduate **ROB COHEN** got his start directing episodes of *Miami Vice, thirtysomething,* and *A Year in the Life*. He moved on to feature films and has directed *Dragon: The Bruce Lee Story, Dragonheart, Daylight, The Skulls, The Fast and the Furious, xXx,* and *Stealth*.

CHRIS COLUMBUS

I'd have to say my favorite film is *On the Waterfront*. It's one of the most dramatic and perfectly constructed pictures I've ever seen. My favorite scene is the final scene on the docks when Karl Malden convinces Brando, who has practically been beaten to death, that if he could walk into the factory and make one last stand then he'll lead the other workers. With everything that has happened to him, Marlon walks into the factory and everyone follows him. It's one of the most rousing scenes ever committed to celluloid. It never fails to inspire me.

ON THE WATERFRONT (1954). Marlon Brando brought a new kind of acting to the screen, and it was dramatically illustrated in Elia Kazan's raw human drama about an ex-boxer who becomes a New York longshoreman and battles corrupt union bosses. His famed "I coulda been somebody" line, spoken to Rod Steiger, is as much a part of cinema history as the brutal black-and-white scenes of what happens to an honest man who resists corruption. Brando's memorable lead performance was swept into the multiple Oscar wins for the picture, director (Kazan), supporting actress (Eva Marie Saint), art direction, cinematography, editing, and screenplay. Also nominated were supporting actors Lee J. Cobb, Karl Malden, and Steiger, along with Leonard Bernstein's score.

Harry Potter auteur **CHRIS COLUMBUS** has directed some of the kiddie classics of all time, including *Home Alone*, *Harry Potter and the Sorcerer's Stone*, and *Harry Potter and the Chamber of Secrets*. The

Ohio native recently directed the big-screen version of *Rent*. Columbus also directed *Adventures in Babysitting*, *Heartbreak Hotel*, *Only the Lonely*, *Home Alone 2: Lost in New York*, *Mrs. Doubtfire*, *Nine Months*, *Stepmom*, and *Bicentennial Man*. He also wrote *Gremlins*, *The Goonies*, *Young Sherlock Holmes*, *Heartbreak Hotel*, *Only the Lonely*, *Nine Months*, and *Christmas with the Kranks*.

RACHAEL LEIGH COOK

My favorite movie is *Say Anything* with John Cusack. I love that one. I just love John Cusack, because he's such a cutie and so endearing. He doesn't try. He just is. He's himself and unapologetic and unassuming. He just seems like a real guy and he's really sensitive. The boom box scene is great, but I liked the dinner table scene even better. John Cusack is sitting there with his girlfriend's father, and he's grilling John about what he does for a living. John says, "I don't want to manufacture anything bought or sold. Or sell anything sold or made." That's my favorite scene. You're really rooting for the couple.

SAY ANYTHING . . . (1989). Writer-director Cameron Crowe specializes in movies about people who don't quite know how to express their love. In this one, John Cusack is the errant suitor trying to prove to Ione Skye that he's really a nice guy, despite her father's (John Mahoney) disapproval. He romances her by lifting a boom box sky-high and playing Peter Gabriel's "In Your Eyes" in her driveway.

RACHAEL LEIGH COOK is a native of Minneapolis, Minnesota, where she began her career as a model. She switched gears to acting and made her debut in *The Baby-Sitters Club*. She has also starred in *She's All That*, *Get Carter*, *Josie and the Pussycats*, *Blow Dry*, *Texas Rangers*, *The House of Yes*, and *Into the West*.

DANE COOK

A staple for me both as a comedy and drama is *Goodfellas*. Sometimes when I watch *Goodfellas*, I say to myself, *Are they still adding more scenes to this movie? Are they still filming?* There are so many brilliant moments that you can't remember each one, so you get something new out of it every single time. I'll actually sit there and go, *No, this has never happened before.* There is just so much to love about that film. As an actor, you learn so many techniques. I watch it from an actor's point of view, a director's point of view, and even the caterer's point of view. I think, *They must have had a delicious lunch that day because those actors are in such a good mood.*

I also love *Planes, Trains & Automobiles*. I'm so into Steve Martin and John Candy. It's such a simple movie with a basic premise. You need to get home to the people you love. It's like a simple song. There are four chords. But you can't get it out of your head.

It's a wonderfully fun movie, but also heartbreaking. When Steve Martin insults John Candy, you can't take it anymore because it's suddenly so painful for him. I also love the ending when you have the turnaround. Steve realizes that John Candy doesn't have a place to be.

That's why you go to the movies. You want to laugh. And you want to feel.

GOODFELLAS (1990). Nobody does Mob violence the way director Martin Scorsese does, and this film version of small-time mobster Henry Hill's true story is a prime example. With Oscar nominations for best picture, director, supporting actress (Lorraine Bracco), editing, and screenplay, it scored only for Joe Pesci, named best supporting actor for his ultraviolent portrait of the viscous Tommy DeVito. Ray Liotta starred as Hill, who eventually ratted out his friends, while Robert De Niro co-starred as a gangster on his way up, no matter what it takes.

PLANES, TRAINS & AUTOMOBILES (1987). John Hughes wrote and directed this story of an ad man named Neal Page (Steve Martin) who must team up with an obnoxious, big-mouthed shower-ring salesman Del Griffith (John Candy) to make the long trek home for Thanksgiving despite complications from traveling.

....

Boston native **DANE COOK** is the nation's hottest rising comic actor whose CD *Retaliation* has gone platinum. He starred in the film *Employee of the Month* and is developing several projects for HBO. He starred with comic Steve Carroll in *Dan in Real Life*.

DAVID CRONENBERG

I don't have one towering film. I can't do it because I'm always missing something else. But I do enjoy *La Dolce vita*, because it really in-
fluenced me. Fellini and Bergman were my role models of what a
director should be. They were directors who even became adjectives.
Movies are now "Fellini-esque" or "Bergman-esque." You can even
say, "I had a 'Fellini-esque experience on the subway.' "

How many modern directors deserve to be adjectives?

These men were authors of their works and expressed a sensibility.
Kid directors today don't even aspire to make *La Dolce vita*. They
would rather have big careers in Hollywood and do *Batman 4*.

La Dolce vita was the first Fellini film I saw, in 1960, and I have
many favorite scenes. I love the famous scene with Sylvia in the fountain. Who doesn't count that as one of their favorites, because it says
so much about so many different things? You also have to consider the
character Mastroianni plays. He longs for beauty and a different life
than he has now. It's such a complex thing and makes it a brilliant
movie.

LA DOLCE VITA (1960). Federico Fellini's masterpiece was a stun-
ner in its day, thanks to a pseudonude scene at the end and the film's
overwhelming sense of ennui among Rome's rich and famous. Marcello Mastroianni's portrait of the world-weary journalist made him
an international star, and the image of Anita Ekberg walking in a
fountain in her evening gown is iconic. Fellini was nominated for his
screenplay and his direction, and the film's art direction also was
mentioned. But its only Oscar was for best costume design.

....

DAVID CRONENBERG hails from Toronto. He started his directing
career as the King of Horror with films such as *Shivers*, *Rabid*, *Scan-
ners*, *Videodrome*, and *The Dead Zone*. He also directed *The Fly*,
Dead Ringers, *Naked Lunch*, *M. Butterfly*, *Crash*, *eXistenZ*, *Spider*,
and *A History of Violence*.

ELISHA CUTHBERT

Fight Club is my favorite movie of all time. I love David Fincher as a director. I like directors who work out of the box. I'm sick of watching boring movies for hours straight. Give me some excitement! Give me something different! Fincher makes it different.

I loved the characters in *Fight Club*. I liked Helena Bonham Carter in it. She was quirky and you didn't know her motives. That kept my interest. I thought that it was also a smart movie, even though it was gory and intense to watch.

The film had a great premise and great twists at the end. I thought it was shot beautifully, too.

Oh, and Brad Pitt is in it.

FIGHT CLUB (1999). Oscar-nominated sound effects are the least important part of David Fincher's complex drama about a drab office type (Edward Norton) who decides he wants a more exciting, aggressive life. That he gets when he hooks up with a soap salesman (Brad Pitt) whose fabulous abs and involvement in an underground "fight club" take him to the brink of self-destruction and exhilaration.

ELISHA CUTHBERT is a native of Calgary who grew up in Quebec, where she began her career as a correspondent for the hit series *Popular Mechanics for Kids*. She's made her mark on the big screen in *Old School*, *Love Actually*, *The Girl Next Door*, and *House of Wax*. Cuthbert also plays Kiefer Sutherland's frequently teary-eyed daughter on the highly rated TV series *24*.

JOHN DAHL

Ace in the Hole is my favorite film directed by Billy Wilder. I think it's a really interesting movie about the convergence of media and morality. And it's Kirk Douglas. Kirk in black-and-white is a gem. Anything he did like that is fine with me.

It's a story about this washed-up New York reporter who ends up in Albuquerque. He's looking for a job, so he takes one at this local newspaper. He's trying to find a way to climb back up to the top, and he goes out to see the rattlesnake festival on the outskirts of town. And they find this man trapped in a cave. Then they have to decide how to get him out. They could get him out by drilling a hole through the top or they could go in another way and get him out quicker. Kirk orchestrates it and says, "Why don't you dig the hole from the top?" He creates a big media circus and carnival around getting this guy out. The man actually dies, and he has to deal with the implications of it.

I like the fact that it's morality coming face-to-face with blind ambition. And he has to pay for the consequences.

It was a flop when it came out, and I'm still scratching my head. How could it be a flop? It's fantastic!

ACE IN THE HOLE (1951). Directed by Billy Wilder, the drama centers on a man trapped underground in a collapsed mine and the reporter who arrives to cover the story. Desperate for a scoop, he takes advantage of the situation, creating a media circus. Kirk Douglas plays the washed-up reporter who goes to work in New Mexico and decides to make himself famous by covering the rescue efforts, with tragic results. Great quote from a character named Lorraine: "I've met a lot of hard-boiled eggs in my time, but you—you're twenty minutes."

....

Montana native **JOHN DAHL** has directed the films *Kill Me Again*, *Red Rock West*, *The Last Seduction*, *Unforgettable*, *Rounders*, *Joy Ride*, and *The Great Raid*.

MATT DAMON

I watch *The Godfather: Part II* at least once a year. Oh God, I like everything about it. The acting is so good that I sit there and wonder if I could ever do anything that great. You look at Pacino and Brando and think, *I've seen this film a hundred times, but it's fresh every single time.*

THE GODFATHER: PART II (1974). Considered by many the best sequel in film history, Francis Ford Coppola's middle movie in the Mario Puzo novel–based trilogy continues the saga of Mafia boss Michael Corleone (Al Pacino) while telling in flashback the story of his father's rise to power in New York's Little Italy. Robert De Niro plays the young Vito Corleone in the Italian language and won a best supporting actor Oscar for his performance. Pacino didn't win for his best actor nomination. Neither did Michael V. Gazzo, Lee Strasberg (supporting actors), Talia Shire (supporting actress), or Theadora Van Runkle (costumer). But the sweeping saga of an Italian family was crowned with Oscars for best picture, art direction, director (Coppola), music, and adapted screenplay.

....

Boston native **MATT DAMON** won a best screenplay Oscar for *Good Will Hunting*, which he wrote with his best friend, Ben Affleck, who was living on his couch. He made his screen debut in *Mystic Pizza* and as an actor has also starred in *School Ties*, *Courage Under Fire*, *The Rainmaker*, *Saving Private Ryan*, *Rounders*, *Dogma*, *The Talented Mr. Ripley*, *The Legend of Bagger Vance*, *All the Pretty Horses*, *Ocean's Eleven*, *Ocean's Twelve*, *The Bourne Identity*, *The Bourne Supremacy*, and *Syriana*. He's starring in the sequels *Ocean's Thirteen* and *The Bourne Ultimatum*.

KRISTIN DAVIS

I love *Groundhog Day*. Start with the fact that I love Bill Murray. He could be in anything and I'd love it, but there is something more here. The film has such a profound message. It says that life is surrendering to the ordinariness of it all. I think that life is like that. You have to celebrate the ordinary.

Bill plays a man who tries to change everything. He has to learn how to surrender and be happy. You have to learn how to cheer people up and do good deeds. That's the way to live a profound and interesting life. But Bill has to learn his lesson in this movie. First, he tries to manipulate Andie MacDowell's character, but when he relaxes, he finally connects with her. It's also so cute at the end when they walk through the snow together after he learns his lesson.

GROUNDHOG DAY (1993). In the catalog of Bill Murray films, this comedy directed by Harold Ramis ranks high, both for its inventiveness and for Murray's audience-pleasing performance as a weatherman who wakes up on Groundhog Day over and over again. Andie MacDowell co-stars as his love interest.

KRISTIN DAVIS made the city pretty sexy in the HBO hit *Sex and the City*, where she played not-always-so-demure art gallery honcho Charlotte York Goldenblatt. The Boulder, Colorado, native graduated from New Jersey's Rutgers University, and immediately hightailed it to New York City after graduation to waitress and audition. She was cast as evil Brooke Armstrong on *Melrose Place* and then later nabbed the role of a lifetime as the uptight but always sweet Charlotte on *Sex and the City*. Davis recently starred in two big-screen kiddie films, *The Adventures of Sharkboy and Lavagirl 3D* and the Disney remake of *The Shaggy Dog*, with Tim Allen. She's not holding her breath for a *Sex and the City* movie.

DANIEL DAY-LEWIS

The first film I ever saw was *Kes*. It remains one of my favorites until this day. I don't even know if it's available on video, but I can tell you that it's a heartbreaking film, because it's about a young boy who is so alone in the world. I felt those same feelings from time to time when I was a young man, and the movie touched those emotions in me.

I think I need to choose a Charles Laughton film too, because he was one of the greatest film actors of all time. No one could touch him. I love *Hobson's Choice*. It's one of those great films about a man who runs a boot maker's shop in Salford. He goes to the pub and tries to deal with his daughters. It's just one of those movies that grips you emotionally, because Charles is so real and you love him.

Now, I must get to the Americans who I saved for last. I'm partial to *A Man for All Seasons*, because Paul Scofield was an amazing actor, and what a beautiful performance. But we can't spend all our time with Paul. I must mention my good friend Martin Scorsese.

What can I say about *Mean Streets*? It's one of my favorite films of all time and the first film I ever saw of Martin's. It was the beginning of my discovery of the whole world of possibilities on the streets of America. I can also sit back and realize now how this film led to *Taxi Driver*, *Raging Bull*, and all the De Niro films.

Oh Christ, how can you even describe it? What happens to you when someone invites you into a world totally unknown to you? It was exotic and dangerous. Martin's world vibrates with life. Johnny Boy is one of the great creations in contemporary film.

But wait, I'm not done. Can I also say *From Here to Eternity* and

On the Waterfront, because Brando was a magnificent man. Robert Duvall is also the master, so I want to mention *Tender Mercies*.

Oh my, I've left the women out of my list. I'd like to add *Sabrina* with Audrey Hepburn. No, wait. Forget that. I want to say *Roman Holiday*. No, wait. Let's put them both down as two of my favorite films because I love her. I love everything about her. She was so beautiful, and when you see her in *Sabrina* or *Roman Holiday*, it's like you're looking at Audrey on the day she was born. She's so fresh and her sense of humor is so bewitching. I love her voice. I love her bearing.

Did others have this many choices?

....

KES (1969). The tagline says it all: "They beat him. They deprived him. They ridiculed him. They broke his heart. But they couldn't break his spirit." Of course, that could describe many childhoods, but this time director Ken Loach filmed a story that centers on young Billy Casper (David Bradley), a poor lad from England who is beaten by his older brother and ignored by everyone around him. His life changes, and he finds love in his life when he discovers a wild kestrel and trains the bird. Watch out for the shocking ending.

HOBSON'S CHOICE (1954). David Lean cast Charles Laughton as Henry Horatio Hobson, a man who runs a booming boot-making shop in Salford, but it's the steps he takes outside of the shop that count the most. Henry must deal with his three daughters, Maggie, Alice, and Vicky, and their various entanglements. It's enough to send any pop down to the local pub.

MEAN STREETS (1973). Martin Scorsese is at his very best in his own New York 'hood. The auteur directed the tale of a small-time hustler named John "Johnny Boy" Civello (Robert De Niro) who must survive life and not get taken out by the other punks on the very mean streets of Little Italy. Harvey Keitel plays Charlie Cappa, a man torn between the staid life of his uncle and the cutting-edge ways of Johnny Boy. An easy choice? Fugghettaboutit.

ON THE WATERFRONT (1954). Marlon Brando brought a new kind of acting to the screen, and it was dramatically illustrated in Elia Kazan's raw human drama about an ex-boxer who becomes a New York longshoreman and battles corrupt union bosses. His famed "I coulda been somebody" line, spoken to Rod Steiger, is as much a part of cinema history as the brutal black-and-white scenes of what happens to an honest man who resists corruption. Brando's memorable lead performance was swept into the multiple Oscar wins for the picture, director (Kazan), supporting actress (Eva Marie Saint), art direction, cinematography, editing, and screenplay. Also nominated were supporting actors Lee J. Cobb, Karl Malden, and Steiger, along with Leonard Bernstein's score.

SABRINA (1954). The lovely Audrey Hepburn begins as the impossibly dowdy Sabrina Fairchild, the chauffeur's daughter, who finds herself and her glow while studying in Paris. When she returns home, two rich men fall at her petite feet, including the pensive, serious Linus Larrabee, played by Humphrey Bogart, and his playboy brother, David Larrabee, whose charm comes in the form of William Holden. Choices, choices. And we're not just talking about her wardrobe.

ROMAN HOLIDAY (1953). So much Audrey, so little time. Screen icon Hepburn won a best actress Oscar, joining designer Edith Head and screenwriters Ian McLellan Hunter and Dalton Trumbo as winners chosen from a long list of nominations for this handsomely photographed black-and-white romance. Set against the backdrop of the Eternal City, it stars Gregory Peck as an unsuspecting reporter who befriends the lovely Hepburn without realizing she's really a princess unable to lead a normal life.

....

English native and Oscar-winning actor **DANIEL DAY-LEWIS** is the son of Cecil Day-Lewis, Poet Laureate of England, and Jill Balcon. His grandfather Sir Michael Balcon founded England's famous Ealing Studios. He won a best actor Oscar for playing Christy Brown in *My Left Foot*. Day-Lewis is considered one of the most talented actors of his generation. Rave reviews followed his roles in *The Last of the Mohicans, The Age of Innocence, In the Name of the Father, The Crucible, The Boxer*, and *Gangs of New York*.

JONATHAN DEMME

Napoleon Dynamite is one of my favorites. It didn't cost any money, but it did something brand new on the big screen that moved me and delighted me.

Oh God, it was just a whole new world. I love the style. I love the performances. My family was obsessed. We saw it so many times together. We still quote the lines from *Napoleon Dynamite*. We're always talking about getting some "sweet moola." That's so funny.

The old classic I like is *Shoot the Piano Player*. I always watch it. It turned me onto cinema as a young major movie fan. It was my first real director's film with a director playing with the medium. It's based on a pulp novel about a piano player. It's a little bit different. The director just took the whole idea of editing and juxtaposing shots, and he did so for the delight of the audience.

NAPOLEON DYNAMITE (2004). Already a cult favorite, Jared Hess's look at the more eccentric members of an Idaho high school is riddled with offbeat laughs. The title character (Jon Heder) lives with his grandmother and answers to a steak-eating uncle while helping boost his friend Pedro's chances of becoming class president. It's a movie that's difficult to describe but easy to enjoy. It won both a Golden Trailer and an MTV Movie Award for best movie in 2005. Heder was a surprise winner for his "election dance" in the Best Musical Performance category and as Breakthrough Male on the MTV event.

SHOOT THE PIANO PLAYER (1960). François Truffaut directed this romantic drama based on the pulp novel by David Goodis. This film is about a shy man (Charles Aznavour) who used to be famous for tickling the ivories. When his wife checks out, he begins to play piano at a run-down Paris bar, where he falls for a waitress.

....

JONATHAN DEMME is one of the most celebrated filmmakers of all time. His early films included *Caged Heat, Crazy Mama, Melvin and Howard, Swing Shift, Stop Making Sense, Something Wild*, and *Married to the Mob*. Demme directed *The Silence of the Lambs*, which won five Oscars, including best picture, best director, best actress for Jodie Foster, best actor for Anthony Hopkins, and best screenplay for Ted Tally. He also directed the critically acclaimed *Philadelphia, Beloved, Bruce Springsteen: The Complete Video Anthology, The Truth About Charlie, The Manchurian Candidate*, and *Neil Young: Heart of Gold*.

JOHNNY DEPP

I grew up loving *The Wizard of Oz*. To tell you the truth, I longed to see the movie again and again because I wanted to go to Oz. I wanted to have a tornado sweep me up and take me away from the life I was living as a teenager. I wished that Auntie Em was my aunt. I didn't have many friends and thought if only I could meet a Tin Man or a Scarecrow that maybe I wouldn't feel alone.

THE WIZARD OF OZ (1939) didn't win the biggest award on Oscar night, but it was nominated for best picture and managed to snag statuettes for its original score and original song, "Over the Rainbow." No one else in the beloved musical—not Judy Garland as Dorothy, the girl from Kansas; not Bert Lahr as the Cowardly Lion; not Ray Bolger as the Scarecrow; and not Jack Haley as the Tin Man—was nominated. The film airs regularly on television as new generations respond to the fantasy tale of a girl spun into the air along with her dog, Toto, and deposited in the Land of Oz. If she wants to get home, she has to "follow the yellow brick road" and go "off to see the Wizard."

....

One of the best actors of his generation, **JOHNNY DEPP** was raised in
Florida. He ventured to Los Angeles to play in bands but began acting
when his friend Nick Cage helped him get an audition for a role in *A
Nightmare on Elm Street*. A star was born. Depp became a teen heart-
throb as cop Tommy Hanson on *21 Jump Street*. His union with director Tim Burton garnered him critical acclaim and resulted in roles in
Edward Scissorhands, *Ed Wood*, and *Charlie and the Chocolate Factory*. He has also received raves for *Finding Neverland* and *Pirates of
the Caribbean: The Curse of the Black Pearl*. His film *Pirates of the
Caribbean: Dead Man's Chest* had the highest-grossing opening week-
end of all time.

ZOOEY DESCHANEL

This is a really hard question because there are so many movies I love. But I'm just going to say *The Philadelphia Story*. What a cast. Cary Grant and Katharine Hepburn. I mean, forget about it! It's just the perfect combination. And then you have the film's script, which again is the perfect combination of light moments and more poignant ones. It's just totally sublime. This brings me to Katharine Hepburn. She's a true original.

I've thought of another favorite during this conversation. I love *The Apartment*. The performances are incredible, plus the movie is funny and touching at the same time. I know that sounds so cheesy. I can't even believe I said "funny" and "touching" in the same sentence. But it is funny and touching. There are so many good parts when you talk about *The Apartment*. The thing is they're all my favorite parts. I'll think of one moment I love . . . and then many other moments flood my mind. But I do love that line "Shut up and deal!"

THE PHILADELPHIA STORY (1940). In George Cukor's comedy version of Philip Barry's play, Katharine Hepburn plays a society dame who dumps her playboy husband (Cary Grant) only to have him turn up at her remarriage to spoil things. James Stewart and Ruth Hussey figure into the action. Stewart won a best actor Oscar for the film which also won one for its screenplay. Nominations also went to Hepburn in the lead, Hussey for support, Cukor, and the film itself.

THE APARTMENT (1960). Billy Wilder's Oscar winner is his somewhat seedy romance about a married boss (Fred MacMurray) who gets a timid employee (Jack Lemmon) to loan him his apartment for trysts with his girlfriend (Shirley MacLaine). Girlfriend and employee fall in love, the boss turns out to be a cad, and movie history was made. The film, director, art direction, screenplay, and editing were Oscar blessed; lead actor and actress Lemmon and MacLaine, supporting thespian Jack Kruschen weren't. The cinematography and sound were also-rans.

....

Eclectic actress **ZOOEY DESCHANEL** received her name straight out of J. D. Salinger's *Franny and Zooey*. The daughter of famed cinematographer Caleb Deschanel got her start in movies with *Almost Famous*. She has since appeared in *The Good Girl, Elf, The Hitchhiker's Guide to the Galaxy, Winter Passing*, and the hit *Failure to Launch* with Matthew McConaughey. She's also an accomplished singer.

VIN DIESEL

I have to say *Gone With the Wind*. I love Clark Gable epics, but there is something more about this one. If you think about it, *Gone With the Wind* really is the first action movie. You have Rhett having to go through this tumultuous time of war. Here is a man who has to transport the people he loves, including his woman, Scarlett. They need to move from one bad location to the next during this time of war with the entire city burning all around them. This was also shot way before the days of computer-generated effects. You can still watch the burning of Atlanta today and marvel at the technical brilliance of this film. You really felt the heat and the danger.

Then you get to the end of the movie and there's more action. Scarlett has to kill the Union men who want to take over her house. Now, there was a woman who was not just beautiful, but she had guts. It's not easy to kill Union soldiers in a hoop skirt.

I love an epic that's laced with love. Has there ever been a better big-screen love story? She wasn't easy, but well worth it. He wasn't easy either, but perfect for her. I have to tell you that I was so in love with Vivien Leigh. She was so beautiful. So perfect. That delicate little face. Gorgeous.

GONE WITH THE WIND (1939). Margaret Mitchell's epic tale of lives and loves scorched by the Civil War became an Oscar-winning classic in the hands of director Victor Fleming. As the fiery Scarlett O'Hara, Vivien Leigh won an Academy Award for best actress, indelibly etching her portrait of a proud Southern belle on the minds of moviegoers. As the dashing Rhett Butler, handsome Clark Gable walked into movie history when he walked out on the troublesome Scarlett, telling her, "Frankly, my dear, I don't give a damn." Hattie McDaniel became the first African American to be nominated for and to win an Oscar (playing Scarlett's maid) in a film that took home statuettes for art direction, cinematography, direction, editing, screenplay, and special technical achievement. Gable lost in the leading male role category, and Olivia de Havilland also lost out as supporting actress for playing the long-suffering Melanie. The film also was bypassed for its special effects, music, and sound.

....

Bald and beautiful action star **VIN DIESEL** is a former New York tough guy and bar bouncer who left college to write and star in his own film about his experiences as an actor, which he called *Multi-Facial*. Spielberg saw the film after it was accepted in the Cannes Film Festival and cast him in *Saving Private Ryan*. Diesel muscled up for the films *Pitch Black*, *The Fast and the Furious*, *Knockaround Guys*, *xXx*, *The Chronicles of Riddick*, and *Find Me Guilty*. He had a huge hit with the kid-friendly *The Pacifier*.

JERRY DOUGLAS

I'll start with *12 Angry Men* because it came from an era of great realism in movies, where Hollywood did classics such as two of the best films ever made, *On the Waterfront* and *Viva Zapata*, and one of my favorite films of all time, *12 Angry Men*.

I like that *12 Angry Men* started out as a play. The script was wonderful, because it showed the vulnerability of the jury system in America. In real life and in this movie, people can't be objective when they're on juries. They bring too much of their own garbage into the jury room, and it affects the case. That's what we see in this film.

Now let's talk about Henry Fonda, who gave an amazing performance, and I think was one of our greatest actors. You never saw him working, which was the key. He's one of my two idols. In fact, I met Henry in the 1970s, and he gave me the best bit of advice in a coffee shop. Of course, it took me ten minutes to gather my nerve to walk up to him and say, "Excuse me, Mr. Fonda. I always love your work." Henry looked at me and said, "I've seen your work, son. You're a good actor." I said, "Thank you, sir." And he said, "Just remember, the work is the star." Good advice. The work was definitely the star in *12 Angry Men*.

I also love *Chariots of Fire*. It's about taking a stand when it comes to your morals and standing up for what you believe in. The movie reminded me of the real-life incident in the 1960s when Sandy Koufax wouldn't pitch on a Jewish holiday. This movie had a heroic man who also stood up for his ideals. This runner wouldn't train on Sundays for religious reasons, because he was a very devout Christian. That's passion.

Both of these are movies about honesty in a world where we have so much dishonesty. These movies stand for the truth and set a good example for our children.

....

12 ANGRY MEN (1957). The power of one man to sway a jury bent on convicting a man based on their preconceptions is what makes Sidney Lumet's Oscar-nominated film a perpetual favorite. Henry Fonda heads the impressive cast that includes Lee J. Cobb, E. G. Marshall, Jack Klugman, Ed Begley, and Jack Warden in bringing the Reginald Rose screenplay to life. Lumet and Rose also were nominated for Academy Awards.

ON THE WATERFRONT (1954). Marlon Brando brought a new kind of acting to the screen, and it was dramatically illustrated in Elia Kazan's raw human drama about an ex-boxer who becomes a New York longshoreman and battles corrupt union bosses. His famed "I coulda been somebody" line, spoken to Rod Steiger, is as much a part of cinema history as the brutal black-and-white scenes of what happens to an honest man who resists corruption. Brando's memorable lead performance was swept into the multiple Oscar wins for the picture, director (Kazan), supporting actress (Eva Marie Saint), art direction, cinematography, editing, and screenplay. Also nominated were supporting actors Lee J. Cobb, Karl Malden, and Steiger, along with Leonard Bernstein's score.

CHARIOTS OF FIRE (1981). Its memorable Vangelis score won an Oscar as did the film about two British track stars, one a Jew (Ben Cross), the other a Scottish missionary (Ian Charleson), who compete in the 1924 Olympics. The stirring drama also won best costume and writing awards. It lost in the categories of best director (Hugh Hudson), supporting actor (Ian Holm), and editing.

·····································

From *Mommy Dearest* with Faye Dunaway to *Avalanche* with Rock Hudson, **JERRY DOUGLAS** has been a character actor for many decades. He also played the handsome heavy on primetime TV in such series as *The Rockford Files, Mission: Impossible, Mannix,* and *Police Story.* He stars as John Abbott on *The Young and the Restless,* the long-running CBS soap opera that has been the number one daytime sudser for the past eighteen years. Jerry says his real claim to fame is his other "role" in real life as a husband to journalist and author Kym Douglas, and father.

FRAN DRESCHER

I have a zillion favorites, but *Annie Hall* is at the top of the list. I found it to be smart, funny, and very insightful about relationships. I love the comparison between Jewish and Gentile families, and the struggle between being considered a serious artist and a sellout in Hollywood.

The film is also about how relationships grow and then ultimately go awry. The message is each person is left with a little piece of the other one. And you remain affected by the relationship forever even though it has dissolved. Ain't that the truth! You move on, but each relationship becomes a passage in your life. I think that's a profound movie message.

I love a smart film like *Annie Hall*. It took me many viewings to catch everything and understand certain references. I also love a movie where you don't get it right away. I'd ask other people, "What do you think they meant by this one line in *Annie Hall*?"

That movie hit bull's-eyes for me. Plus it was shot in New York. What else do ya want?

ANNIE HALL (1977). "La-dee-dah" entered cinema lexicon when star Diane Keaton said it in Woody Allen's Oscar-winning film. Director Allen and his leading lady also picked up Academy Awards for the quirky romantic comedy about a New York comedian with as many hang-ups as his girlfriend has. Allen and Marshall Brickman took home screenwriting honors as well for the film that became a fashion trendsetter, thanks to Keaton's baggy pants and vests.

• •

Noo yawker **FRAN DRESCHER** with her trademark nasal whine began her film career getting her boogey on with John Travolta on the dance floor in *Saturday Night Fever*. On television, she was the flashy girl from Flushing as *The Nanny*.

RICHARD DREYFUSS

Do you want one or two or my list? Okay, I'll give you the list. I'll start with *A Few Good Men*. I just get stuck in that movie—caught—whenever it's on. You can't get much better than that courtroom scene at the end. It's also an intelligentally written movie, and I appreciate when the words matter. I also love *Gone With the Wind* because it's an epic romance. And I can't leave you without saying *Citizen Kane*. It's the classic of all classics. Mesmerizing! You feel wrong turning it off if you happen upon *Citizen Kane* on cable. It's just gorgeous filmmaking. And it meets my test, which is can you stick with the film. I'm stuck when it comes to *Citizen Kane*.

A FEW GOOD MEN (1992) is Rob Reiner's critically acclaimed film written by Aaron Sorkin. It revolves around a military lawyer, played by Tom Cruise, who defends two military grunts accused of killing an enlisted man. They were operating under the orders of Colonel Nathan R. Jessep, played by Jack Nicholson. The film culminates in Nicholson screaming at Cruise: "The truth. You can't handle the truth!" The movie also stars Demi Moore and Kevin Bacon.

   CITIZEN KANE (1941) is often referred to as one of the greatest movies of all time. It's Orson Welles's classic, written by Herman J. Mankiewicz, about a publishing tycoon named Charles Foster Kane, who utters the word "Rosebud" on his deathbed. The rest of the movie is told in flashback as those around him unravel the mystery of his final word. The character is based on newspaper magnet William Randolph Hearst. It won an Oscar for original screenplay.

GONE WITH THE WIND (1939). Margaret Mitchell's epic tale of lives and loves scorched by the Civil War became an Oscar-winning classic in the hands of director Victor Fleming. As the fiery Scarlett O'Hara, Vivien Leigh won an Academy Award for best actress, indelibly etching her portrait of a proud Southern belle on the minds of moviegoers. As the dashing Rhett Butler, handsome Clark Gable walked into movie history when he walked out on the troublesome Scarlett, telling her, "Frankly, my dear, I don't give a damn." Hattie McDaniel became the first African American to be nominated for and to win an Oscar (playing Scarlett's maid) in a film that took home statuettes for art direction, cinematography, direction, editing, screenplay and special technical achievement. Gable lost in the leading male role category, and Olivia de Havilland also lost out as supporting actress for playing the long-suffering Melanie. The film also was bypassed for its special effects, music, and sound.

....

Born in Brooklyn and raised in Beverly Hills, **RICHARD DREYFUSS** began his film career with a small role in *The Graduate*. He went on to star in American classics, including *American Graffiti, Jaws, Close Encounters of the Third Kind, The Goodbye Girl, Down and Out in Beverly Hills, Stand by Me, Stakeout,* and *Mr. Holland's Opus*.

MINNIE DRIVER

Golly gee, it would have to be *Tootsie*. Oh my God. Every single element of that film, from Bill Murray to Dustin Hoffman to Sydney Pollack to Jessica Lange to Teri Garr, is so perfect. I love the first time you see Dustin Hoffman in the getup. He's silly and funny, but also lovely as Dorothy. You almost wish there really were two people, because as much as you want Dustin to get together with Jessica, you want Dorothy to exist and live on as her friend. I think we all want a friend like Dorothy. And I love the sweet crush that Jessica's father has on Dorothy. You feel so sad for him, because his heart is right out there.

More than anything, too, *Tootsie* talks about how life can be difficult for an actor. How you have to really put yourself out there for a role. How it's heartbreaking when you can't get work. I think there is a little Tootsie in all of us.

....

TOOTSIE (1982). Dustin Hoffman embraced his inner (and outer woman) as an actor who is desperate to get a role, so he dresses up like a woman and is cast on a popular TV soap opera. Hoffman played the dual role of Michael Dorsey/Dorothy Michaels—and frankly it's hard to imagine that Dorothy isn't a real person, because we need her more than we need him. The excellent supporting cast includes Teri Garr, Bill Murray, Charles Durning, and Jessica Lange, who won a best actress in a supporting role Oscar for playing a soap actress who is mentored by Dorothy and finds she has an attraction to her at the same time.

....

London native **MINNIE DRIVER** made her mark as overweight lassie Benny in the heartwarming Irish drama *Circle of Friends*. She has also starred in *Golden Eye, Grosse Pointe Blank, Good Will Hunting, The Governess, An Ideal Husband, Return to Me, Beautiful,* and *The Phantom of the Opera,* for which she did her own singing—to rave reviews.

DAVID DUCHOVNY

I love *Chinatown*. It's just a perfectly written movie with a clear-cut beginning, middle, and end. I remember the first time I saw it, and I just sat there in the theater, completely absorbed. I couldn't decide what was better—the screenplay, the acting, the direction. Now that's a winning movie—when you can't decide which is the best part because it's all the best part.

Above all, it's a smart story. How many times do we ever get a smart story? Right there they had me.

I love a story, too, about Los Angeles. For some reason that city has such a romantic draw, and here you have a story about L.A. and how it really became L.A. Fascinating. I like any movie with a history behind it. I think Roman Polanski really takes you inside early L.A. and makes you feel like you're in that place at that specific time.

And then you have Jack. What else can you say? Jack is Jack. He's always magic.

CHINATOWN (1974). California's tangled history of trying to find water for its desert climate was just the backdrop screenwriter Robert Towne and director Roman Polanski needed for their equally tangled love story. Jack Nicholson is Jake "J.J." Gittes, a private investigator looking into an adultery case, who finds out that there is more than meets his private eye. Faye Dunaway plays a woman with quite a past. John Huston loomed large as the mastermind behind an elaborate plot to buy cheap water to cultivate arid land and sell it at top price. Towne won an Oscar for his intricate screenplay, but the film failed to score more than nominations for best picture, director, actor (Nicholson), actress (Dunaway), art direction, cinematography, score, sound, editing, and costumes. Line to love: Walsh — "Forget it, Jake. It's Chinatown."

....

Cerebral star **DAVID DUCHOVNY** went the academic route at Princeton University and then earned a graduate degree in English literature at Yale. Between exams, he was on a bus to New York City to study acting. He played Fox Mulder on the hit series *The X Files* for nine years and has also appeared in movies such as *Full Frontal, Zoolander, Return to Me, Connie and Carla*, and *Trust the Man*. He also directed the drama *House of D*, starring his wife, Téa Leoni.

KIMBERLY ELISE

I'm from Minnesota and I consider my teenage years a magical time in my life. Nothing was better than the first time I saw *Purple Rain*, starring Prince in his own hometown, and mine, in Minnesota.

I'll never forget that I was in junior high. There was so much excitement around town that Prince was making this big movie. Now, I love Prince and always admired his music.

I'll never forget that I was counting down the days until the movie opened. Any little bit of information about the film that you could read in the paper was like a little treasure. Then all of a sudden, I was standing in line, getting my ticket, and it was just magical. I sat in that theater with Prince's music all around me. It was a major sensation.

I didn't want the film to be over. In fact, I saw it again right away. Even now if it's on, I don't care what I'm doing. I sit down and watch *Purple Rain*. We're talking triple digits. That's how many times I've seen it. Now, it's a nostalgic thing for me that reminds me of my childhood. I could do all of the dialogue right now if you want me to do it.

Come on, I really could do it.

PURPLE RAIN (1984). Rock impressario Prince surprised critics with his well-made autobiographical musical about a would-be star trying to escape the shadow of his father's destructive behavior. Real-life Prince associates Apollonia and Morris Day co-star in the film that won Prince an Oscar for best original score.

....

Beautiful **KIMBERLY ELISE** grew up in Minneapolis, Minnesota, and later attended the American Film Institute. She made her big screen debut in *Set It Off* and then played Denver, Oprah Winfrey's daughter, in *Beloved*. Other film roles include *Bait*, *John Q*, *Women Thou Art Loosed*, *The Manchurian Candidate*, and *Diary of a Mad Black Woman*.

PETER AND
BOBBY FARRELLY

PETER FARRELLY:

I'm sure this movie is not for everybody, but I just love *Something Wild*. I love that movie. It's just one of those films that strikes a chord. I love the way it looks. I love how New York looks and how the country-side looks. In every movie I've done I tried to capture that look. It's a good goal because our movies have a lot of road trips in them.

Something Wild captures little parts of Americana that are not clichéd. It's real. Jeff Daniels's performance is one of the great ones of all time. He's funny and complicated. It was also one of Ray Liotta's first movies. And Melanie Griffith was really great. Demme directed it, and I could watch it over and over.

Once, I actually drove to Albuquerque from Los Angeles to go to a wedding. I left at five in the morning to get there at six at night and drove straight through. I got six tickets. It's probably a national record. I got one in California, four in Arizona, two in New Mexico. That's how fast I was driving to get to this wedding. But then I got to the hotel and flipped on the TV and *Something Wild* was just beginning. I sat on the bed and watched the whole movie. I even missed the wedding but snuck into the reception. After that amazing effort to be on time, that film stopped me cold.

The movie is not for everyone. I have a friend who hates it, but that's just his opinion.

I love the part where Jeff Daniels, who plays this straight-laced, uptight businessman, has lunch at this diner and tries to skip out on the bill on purpose. My friend who hates the movie saw that part and said, "F— him. I hate this movie." Now, I'm not condoning all of this, but the scene made me curious. I don't like a guy who hops out of a restaurant. But I do like a guy who has many sides.

Melanie sees that he has this whole other side and exploits it. And then you have Ray Liotta who is crazy nuts. He's the perfect bully with a charming side. He stops at the Roadhouse Motel. There's a girl in the gift shop. He's got Melanie in the room scared to death, and he ends up sleeping with the girl at the shop. He's unbelievably creepy.

By the way, this movie is the reason we hired Jeff Daniels for *Dumb & Dumber*. I begged the studio to let us have Jeff. I saw *Something Wild* six years before, but the guys at New Line doing *Dumb & Dumber* said, "No, we have Jim Carrey and Jeff is not a comic actor." I said, "Watch *Something Wild*. He's hilarious. He's a great actor." They watched it and we hired him.

BOBBY FARRELLY:

This goes to show where my head is. I was going to talk about one of our movies!

My favorite movie from someone else was *Jaws*. I can never forget the impact it had on me in the theater. I wouldn't go to a swimming pool for a year. It's amazing that a movie could do that. I didn't know a movie could have that kind of power.

What fascinates me is even now, close to thirty years later, it's still an amazing movie. Now if the movie was made it would be CGI and stupid and all fake. They would never do it as well as Spielberg did it then. He even killed off the hero. You didn't want Quint, played by Robert Shaw, to die, but he died doing what he loved to do, which was trying to get that shark. It was noble, but gory. But it was cool that he died.

So much of it was what you didn't see, and the orchestra represented the shark. I love the hint of it. The shark would come and sometimes it never came. By the way, at the end of that first summer when it came out, I didn't see it forty times. I probably only went three or four times. But I could still do every line in that movie. I could quote them today. I still remember so many of them.

Forget about that pool comment. I couldn't even bathe for a year.

....

SOMETHING WILD (1986). Melanie Griffith lived up to the title playing a wild woman who seduces a straight-arrow type (Jeff Daniels) only to have things take a dangerous turn when the duo runs into her ex-con hubby (Ray Liotta). Jonathan Demme directed Liotta in a part that saddled him with these psycho roles for life.

JAWS (1975). When director Steven Spielberg took on Peter Benchley's bestselling novel about a shark attacking people off the shores of Amity Island, the term "summer blockbuster" was created, forever changing the way movies were released. With improvised special effects, Spielberg made people literally afraid to go back into the water, and Benchley spent the later years of his life trying to restore the good image of great white sharks. John Williams's famed score was Oscar rewarded as were the film's sound and editing. But the film itself lost in the best picture category.

....

PETER AND BOBBY FARRELLY never met a gross joke that they thought was just too gross. The Pennsylvania natives directed and produced *Dumb & Dumber*, starring Jim Carrey; *Kingpin*, starring Woody Harrelson; *There's Something About Mary*, starring Cameron Diaz; *Me, Myself & Irene*, starring Carrey; *Shallow Hal*, starring Jack Black and Gwyneth Paltrow; *Stuck on You*, starring Matt Damon; and *Fever Pitch*, starring Drew Barrymore. They're currently developing a big-screen adventure for The Three Stooges.

JON FAVREAU

I'll go on the record to say *The Blues Brothers*. It's such a fun movie, and it took my favorite actors of that time and put them in a big, big movie that had a lot of excitement and enthusiasm. There was also a lot of affection for Chicago.

I thought I knew Chicago from this one film, which was really like a big love letter to the city. You saw the bridges, the Picasso statue, Wrigley Field. It was a movie with a sightseeing tour.

I love the chase scene, because it had all the action and all the humor. You could tell Dan and John were having crazy fun making the movie, and all their friends are in there, too. You see Carrie Fisher and John Candy.

One more thing. John Belushi was a real comedy inspiration to me. How gutsy to do a whole movie where you only take your sunglasses off for a minute. He plays the movie behind those glasses.

And best of all, you have a movie here about a summer band that became one of the classic films of all time. You couldn't plan that one. It just happened—and I'm so happy that it did.

THE BLUES BROTHERS (1980). John Landis wrote this perennial comedy favorite with co-star Dan Aykroyd, who, along with fellow *Saturday Night Live* comedian John Belushi, adopted the personas of a pair of superhip blues aficionados, Jake and Elwood Blues. They set out to save the Catholic orphanage in which they were raised, and the rest is movie comedy history. Aykroyd, along with the late Belushi's brother, Jim, still make appearances as the Blue Brothers, mostly for private conventions.

....

JON FAVREAU is an alum of Chicago's ImprovOlympics, where he learned comedy with Chris Farley and Mike Myers. He began his career as an actor and logged roles in *Rudy, Batman Forever, Swingers, Deep Impact, Very Bad Things, Love & Sex, The Replacements, Made, Daredevil, The Big Empty, Elf, Something's Gotta Give, Wimbledon*, and *The Break-Up*. He stepped behind the camera to direct *Made, Elf*, and *Zathura*.

AMERICA FERRERA

A classic I love so much is *Now and Then*. It has that great quality of really telling the truth about young girls, and it focuses on great friendships. I remember seeing it with my friends. We were in a dark theater going, "I'm here. You're here. No, you're the other girl." We were all trying to live one of the characters in the movie.

I was the one with the big boobs because that kinda worked!

My friends and I saw it over and over again. I have three best friends, too, so it just hit me in the heart. It's like we're a sisterhood, and that film gave me that sisterhood feeling.

I love movies about what it is to be young and excited. I love films about special relationships and what it means to be alive. *Now and Then* made you want to be friends with those girls. Now we have *Sex and the City*. But I want to know the girls from *Now and Then*.

NOW AND THEN (1995). It's girl power all the way when four childhood friends—Melanie Griffith, Rita Wilson, Rosie O'Donnell, and Demi Moore—reunite to remember a special summer when they were twelve. The film flashes back to the women as preteens in the 1970s. The girls are played by Christina Ricci, Thora Birch, Gaby Hoffmann, and Ashleigh Aston Moore. Cloris Leachman played Grandma Albertson.

••••••••••••••••••••••••••••••••••

Los Angeles resident **AMERICA FERRERA** is the youngest of six kids. She made her mark in community theater and school plays auditioning for movie roles. America charmed audiences with her breakthrough role in the film *Real Women Have Curves*. Her follow-up roles included *Darkness Minus Twelve, Plainsong, How the Garcia Girls Spent Their Summer, The Sisterhood of the Traveling Pants*, and *Lords of Dogtown*.

50 CENT

Oh baby, I got so many movies that I enjoy. I'm a man on the road. Just gimme a DVD player and a great movie and I'm happy. But if I had to pick my favorite one, I love *Friday*. I could sit down and watch it right now. I could watch it anytime. That movie makes me laugh. And I'm a big fan of Chris Tucker. I just love how Ice Cube and Chris Tucker get themselves in and out of so much trouble. It cracks me up to watch them interact. And no disrespect to Cube, but Chris Tucker is my man. He's such an incredible comedian. Just the looks on his face. I'm gonna laugh just thinking about it.

FRIDAY (1995). Rapper Ice Cube co-wrote and took the lead role of Craig Jones in this story of two guys, Craig and Smokey (Chris Tucker), who hang out on a Friday afternoon, smoking, drinking, and dealing with the ladies while hiding from a drug dealer and navigating the hardships of the 'hood.

Internationally famous rapper-turned-actor **50 CENT** (real name Curtis Jackson) survived the tough streets of South Jamaica, Queens. His story served as the basis for the semiautobiographical and controversial film *Get Rich or Die Tryin'*, in which he played Marcus. The film depicts how in real life he was shot nine times and survived. His debut album sold 900,000 copies in one week.

NAOMI FONER

I always say *Jules and Jim*. It was just very personally affecting to me. I remember when François Truffaut died, I pulled my car over to the side of a freeway and I cried like I knew him. I never met him.

I did this because I think that movie does the best thing movies can do. It opened up possibilities for me. It said everything didn't have to be done one way—both in form and content. It moved me in some primal way, and I felt very changed by seeing it.

I can't tell you about a favorite scene. It was just the whole essence of it. There is the idea that you don't have to be predictable. You don't have to do what's expected. There is joy in taking the other path. There is nothing really logical about why I love it. It just made me feel I didn't have to be what other people wanted me to be.

That's the kind of work I aspire to. The best movies move people and make them think about things. Maybe they'll do something differently.

....

JULES AND JIM (1962) is the François Truffaut classic of a love triangle between two friends and a woman who lives by her impulses. The film defined the lush beauty of French cinema for those unfamiliar with the art. Oskar Werner played Jules while Henri Serre was Jim, with Jeanne Moreau as the beautiful Catherine. Line to quote: Jim— "We played with life and lost."

....

Screenwriter **NAOMI FONER** is a New York native and alumna of Barnard College. A former producer of the award-winning children's

TV series *The Electric Company*, she is better known for writing stirring screenplays about family, including *Violets Are Blue*, *Running on Empty*, *A Dangerous Woman*, *Losing Isaiah*, and *Bee Season*. She has also written a screenplay based on the life of *Peyton Place* author Grace Metalious to star Sandra Bullock. Naomi is also proud mom to actors Jake and Maggie Gyllenhaal.

JAMES FRANCO

Rushmore is it for me. I just think it's one of the smartest comedies I've ever seen. The filmmakers put so much detail into building that world. Plus, it's fun to go back and look for all those details you miss during the first few viewings.

I have to tell you that I love Bill Murray. I love the little plays he puts on in the movie. They're just fantastic. When they put on *Serpico* as a play, it's awesome. Then backstage, Bill tells someone, "You skipped a line. Don't mess with my play." They have a little fight over it, and each time I just crack up. It's my favorite film.

RUSHMORE (1998). Wes Anderson's penchant for oddball movies was cemented with this entry about a student from Rushmore prep school who loves the place and heads its extracurricular activities but can't seem to do well in class. When he and a fellow student's father fall for the same elementary school teacher, things get complicated. Jason Schwartzman, son of actress Talia Shire and nephew of director Francis Ford Coppola, stars, along with Bill Murray and Olivia Williams.

Intense young actor **JAMES FRANCO** is a Palo Alto, California, native who was so shy that he studied acting at UCLA to become a little bit more outgoing. He left school after a year and studied at Robert Carnegie's Playhouse West. Franco got his big break on TV's cult hit *Freaks and Geeks*. He has also starred in the movies *Never Been Kissed*, *Whatever It Takes*, *Annapolis*, and *City by the Sea*, for which

Robert De Niro handpicked him to play his druggie son in the gritty urban tale. Franco received acclaim for his TNT's *James Dean*. He didn't get his wish to play *Spider-Man*, a role that went to Tobey Maguire. But Franco's audition was so good that he became Spidey's best friend, Harry Osborn, in the series of hit movies. Franco is also an accomplished painter.

MORGAN FREEMAN

This is such a hard choice, but I'm thinking that more and more my all-time favorite movie is Baz Luhrmann's *Moulin Rouge!* It's that kind of movie where you can kick back and just enjoy. Everything about it is outstanding. Forget saying that it's to die for. It's to cry for. I've never seen anything done quite that well.

MOULIN ROUGE! (2001). The dazzling Nicole Kidman was nominated for a best actress Oscar for her role as doomed Satine in the drama, musical, and love story directed by Baz Luhrmann. The story focuses on a poet, played by Ewan McGregor, who falls head over heels for a gorgeous courtesan who is promised to an angry and jealous duke (Richard Roxburgh). The story unfolds at the legendary Paris club Moulin Rouge in 1899. John Leguizamo gives an inspired turn as Toulouse-Lautrec. The biggest surprise in the movie was that McGregor could hit the high notes.

Dignified and graceful actor **MORGAN FREEMAN** has been called the greatest actor of our times. He grew up in Memphis and served as a mechanic in the U.S. Air Force. He began his career playing Easy Reader on the hit children's TV series *The Electric Company*. His early films included *Eyewitness, Harry & Son, Teachers, Street Smart,* which earned him an Oscar nomination, *Clean and Sober, Lean on Me,* and *Driving Miss Daisy,* which earned him another Oscar nod. He has also starred in *Unforgiven* and *The Shawshank Redemption,* where his role as Red earned him a third Oscar nomination. Other roles include *Kiss the Girls, Amistad, Se7en, Along Came a Spider, The Sum of All Fears, Bruce Almighty*, and *Batman Begins*. He won a best supporting actor Oscar for his role as a washed-up fighter in *Million Dollar Baby*.

STEPHEN GAGHAN

I'm one of those people who loves Z, by Costa-Gavras. I like the way the political aspect of that film is humanized. The movie starts with these guys talking about a mold or a rot on the leaves. Slowly, you realize the man is talking about the fear of socialism. He's making this analogy. It's a rot.

Then the camera shows you the balding hairlines of these men. Their paunches. You're like, *Why is there all this rhetoric. This makes no sense.* But then you look at these people carefully and you know exactly who they are.

You have a great military leader who has killed, but he's the hope. We watch him look in the window of a hair salon. He sees a beautiful woman and imagines an affair. Suddenly, the movie goes off in that direction.

Basically, the movie says that the big dog gets to do whatever he wants. Even if someone is a great man and a great leader, oh yeah, he can still be cheating on his wife. That's a very courageous thing to do in a movie, because many movies just create perfect people.

I think the ending is unbelievably powerful. When the Z is drawn in the street, you realize there's a long-term struggle going on. The world is composed of ideas and some are dangerous ideas.

This movie is so applicable to these times. Just like in Z, there is an ideological battle going on out there and many of us are in the middle. Just like in Z, you have to be really certain what you stand for and that your house is clean. Otherwise, there is hypocrisy.

••••••••••••••••••••••••••••••••••

Z (1969). Costa-Gavras's Oscar-winning film is a masterpiece of sharp editing that chronicles the democratic Greek government overthrow by right-wing military figures and police. Its editing won an Oscar, and the film also picked up nominations for its director, its screenplay, and as best picture, a rare honor considering it also competed and won as best foreign language film. Based on a true story, Z is based on the aftermath of Grigoris Lambrakis's assassination and the subsequent military junta. The film was so controversial that it was originally banned in Greece.

••••••••••••••••••••••••••••••••••

STEPHEN GAGHAN is an acclaimed screenwriter who recently stepped behind the camera to direct *Syriana*. As a writer, he is known for tough, gritty material, including *Rules of Engagement*, *Traffic*, *Abandon*, *The Alamo*, and *Havoc*.

RICHARD GERE

The Passenger has always been one of my favorite films. It kind of captured an era of Michelangelo Antonioni and Harold Pinter. These were dominant forces in how we expressed what was going on. There was a sense of disconnect in the world when these men made films. There was a sense of menace. There was a sense of us being small cogs in a large wheel.

This movie reminded me that there are mysteries here that have to be explored. Identity. Is there a self? Who am I? Can I get out of this bondage of self? *The Passenger* is all about that, and he does it so economically that you're not even aware he's saying it to you.

There are wonderful shots in that movie. I remember those shots, and I haven't seen this movie in twenty years. There are shots that I can remember in detail and wonderful scenes. One of my favorite scenes is one with the rebel prince. He's interviewing him and then turns the camera on him. Brilliant. That's one of my favorite scenes in one of my favorite films.

THE PASSENGER (1975) is Michelangelo Antonioni's drama about a reporter, played by Jack Nicholson, who is going through an identity crisis while being stuck in North Africa to write about the Civil War and guerrilla freedom fighters. When the man staying in the hotel room next door to him accidentally dies, Nicholson assumes the identity of the corpse and begins a new life while those closest to him are told he has died. The film also stars Maria Schneider as a young architecture student who is backpacking her way through Spain.

RICHARD GERE   91

Deep-thinking actor and humanitarian **RICHARD GERE** grew up in
Philly. His career began with *Looking for Mr. Goodbar, Days of
Heaven, Bloodbrothers*, and *Yanks*. He has also starred in his own clas-
sics, including *American Gigolo, An Officer and a Gentleman, Pretty
Woman*, and the Oscar-winning *Chicago*, for which he learned to
sing and tap. Just don't ask him to do it in public now.

TERRY GILLIAM

One-Eyed Jacks. Come on! When that film came out I was on 42nd Street in New York when we still had double bills. I was about twenty-three, and I just sat there in this old theater and said, "GREAT! Bring on Brando!" But first, I had to sit through this crap movie to get to *One-Eyed Jacks*. It was torture!

As for *One-Eyed Jacks*, I love it and still love it. It's some of the greatest stuff Brando ever did. Ugh! Elmo the cage rotter with his great gut sticking out! Come on! Please. I love it. I love that movie. I've seen it more times than every movie I've ever watched and now I want the world to rediscover *One-Eyed Jacks*.

You want specifics? First, let me stay it's great right from the beginning, when Brando is sitting there and they're robbing a bank. He's eating food and fiddling around. He talks to the girls. There is that lovely moment where he steals the ring and then rushes off to the girl he is trying to seduce. He tells her a story about her mother. And then when the boys yell, "We gotta get out of here," he's prying the ring off his finger. It's just brilliant stuff!

ONE-EYED JACKS (1961). Marlon Brando directed and stars as Rio in this screen Western. Rio is a bank robber on the lam after he pulls a heist in New Mexico. Karl Malden is Dad Longworth, who steals the gold and leaves Rio to be captured by the law. Rio gets out of the pokey and decides to ride for revenge. The only problem is that Dad Longworth is now a California sheriff who is waiting for Rio to return. Slim Pickens is Deputy Lon Dedrick.

....

Hollywood visionary **TERRY GILLIAM** was a founding member of Monty Python with John Cleese, Eric Idle, and Graham Chapman. Their first feature film was *And Now for Something Completely Different*. It was only a prelude to their medieval classic *Monty Python and the Holy Grail*, co-directed by Gilliam. Their other films include *Life of Brian* and *The Meaning of Life*. On his own, Gilliam directed the fantasy film *Jabberwocky* and then the hit *Time Bandits*. He earned an Oscar nomination for best screenplay for his film *Brazil*. He also directed the acclaimed *The Fisher King* with Robin Williams and Jeff Bridges, *The Adventures of Baron Munchausen*, *Twelve Monkeys*, *Monty Python & the Quest for the Holy Grail*, *Fear and Loathing in Las Vegas*, and *The Brothers Grimm*.

AKIVA GOLDSMAN

It's geeky to say it, but my favorite movie is probably, *It's a Wonderful Life*. When I watch films over and over again, they usually cease to be effective. But that never happens with this film.

I'm also really good at not seeing the whole movie. I watch the scenes. I see the nails and the thumbtacks. I'm a writer, so that's what I see. I don't do that with *It's a Wonderful Life*. I don't see the thumbtacks and the seams. This movie absorbs me and transports me. I'm grateful for that fact.

I still cry when Zuzu says, "Every time a bell rings, an angel gets his wings." But I also cry at Budweiser commercials.

IT'S A WONDERFUL LIFE (1946). If you haven't seen this Frank Capra movie at Christmastime, you don't own a television set. A perpetual holiday favorite, the beloved Capra movie never won an Oscar, but it has captured the hearts of audiences drawn to its morality tale of a man (James Stewart) who wants to end his life because of his many problems when his guardian angel (Henry Travers) tells him what life would be like if he never existed. The film was nominated for best picture, director, actor, editing, and sound.

....

AKIVA GOLDSMAN wrote the screenplay for *The Da Vinci Code* and won a best screenplay Oscar for *A Beautiful Mind*. The award-winning screenwriter also penned *Cinderella Man; I, Robot; Practical Magic; A Time to Kill; Batman Forever; Silent Fall;* and *The Client.* He also produced *Poseidon, Mr. & Mrs. Smith, Starsky & Hutch, Deep Blue Sea,* and *Constantine.*

ALYSON HANNIGAN

I truly believe the film *Say Anything* ruined real-life romance for all women of my generation. I left that movie thinking that all guys should look like John Cusack and, frankly, they should be standing on the end of my driveway with a boom box. But did I get a boom box in high school? There wasn't even an accidental boom box or even a loud radio coming my way.

They weren't John Cusack, who was always so smart and cute in movies while most boys were dorks. Plus, you don't want to put pressure on the guy, but just calling would have been nice. I know, I know, us girls. We ask for so much.

SAY ANYTHING . . . (1989). Writer-director Cameron Crowe specializes in movies about people who don't quite know how to express their love. In this one, John Cusack is the errant suitor trying to prove to Ione Skye that he's really a nice guy, despite her father's (John Mahoney) disapproval. He romances her by lifting a boom box sky high and playing Peter Gabriel's "In Your Eyes" in her driveway.

ALYSON HANNIGAN was born in Washington, D.C., but also lived in Atlanta and Los Angeles. At age four, she was already acting in commercials for McDonald's, Six Flags, and Oreos. A series regular on TV's *Buffy the Vampire Slayer*, she has also logged movie roles in *American Pie*, *American Pie 2*, *American Wedding*, *Boys and Girls*, and *Date Movie*. She currently stars in the CBS series *How I Met Your Mother*.

WOODY HARRELSON

My favorite film is probably a Paul Newman movie called *Cool Hand Luke*. That's a great movie about a guy against the system. He will not give up. I love movies like that because they inspire me to be a better man. I also love *Norma Rae*, because it's a little person against the system.

My other favorite film is *Harold and Maude*. It's one of the most beautiful love stories ever told. Just the relationship between the two tells you everything that's wonderful about life. There's poetry in the dialogue. I think it's one of the all-time great, genius movies.

And I love the scene where Harold and Maude are together, and the line is something like, "There will always be glorious ducks." Ruth Gordon says it. It's just a real gem of a line.

COOL HAND LUKE (1967). George Kennedy received a best supporting actor Oscar, but Paul Newman was bypassed for his lead performance in what is considered a defining role in his career, that of the indomitable Lucas Jackson, a prisoner who wouldn't stay put. With Oscar nominations for its music and adapted screenplay, the prison drama has an all-star cast, featuring Harry Dean Stanton, Strother Martin, Dennis Hopper, and Joe Don Baker.

....

WOODY HARRELSON grew up in Lebanon, Ohio, but began his career on stage in New York. He wasn't hitting the boards for long because soon he was starring as dim-bulb bartender Woody on the hit TV series *Cheers*. His film roles include *White Men Can't Jump*, *Indecent Proposal*, *Natural Born Killers*, *North Country*, and *A Prairie Home Companion*.

JOSH HARTNETT

When I was a kid, my dad was obsessed with Monty Python. He made me watch it with him, and I loved it. All of those Python films were just good, goofy fun, plus those guys were so funny individually. When you put them together, it was just outstanding. They're geniuses. You just have to watch *The Holy Grail* for proof.

The other film I love is *The Big Lebowski*. It's Jeff Bridges as The Dude. He's just so good that I bow down to him. Jeff Bridges is that character, but he's not playing the same guy he has played in other films. He just became The Dude. I don't know how he did it, but he just transcended the character. He makes you think that Dude guy really exists. You wish you could meet him and go have a White Russian with him. Can you imagine having a drink with The Dude?

I also love *The Sting*. It's one of the most interestingly directed movies of all time. The script is beautiful, too. All of that Robert Shaw dialogue is perfect. The scene I always love the best is the one where Paul Newman is playing poker on the train. He's a drunk guy or playing a drunk guy and he looks like he's having the time of his life. I want to be in that train car with him. That film is a classic with a surreal feel to it.

MONTY PYTHON AND THE HOLY GRAIL (1975). Terry Gilliam directs Graham Chapman, John Cleese, Eric Idle, Terry Jones, Michael Palin, and himself in the story of King Arthur and his knights searching for the Holy Grail.

THE BIG LEBOWSKI (1998). Here's a typical Joel and Ethan

Coen movie, this one about Los Angeles slacker Dude Lebowski (Jeff Bridges) being mistaken for a millionaire of the same name. The poor Lebowski wants some restitution for a rug because a pair of gangsters urinated on it, and, well, that's how a Coen Brothers movie goes.

THE STING (1973). Two con men (Paul Newman and Robert Redford) take on a Mob boss (Robert Shaw) in the Oscar-winning George Roy Hill film about getting even. There are twists and turns galore as the cons try to outsmart the man who murdered a friend, and the film was richly rewarded with Oscars for its director, costumes, art direction, music (with its familiar piano-tinkling theme song by Marvin Hamlisch), and screenplay. Redford, the film's cinematography, and its sound were also-rans at the Oscars.

....

Midwest hunk **JOSH HARTNETT** grew up in Minneapolis and then attended SUNY in Purchase, New York. With his sights on acting, Hartnett did a quick stint on the TV series *Cracker* before breaking into movies with roles in *Halloween H2O*, *Pearl Harbor*, *The Virgin Suicides*, *The Faculty*, *Black Hawk Down*, *40 Days and 40 Nights*, and *The Black Dahlia*.

SALMA HAYEK

Oh, there are so many films I love. Oh my God, how will I answer this question? I'll tell you a funny one that means so much to me. I just love the original *Willy Wonka & the Chocolate Factory*. That film is what made me want to be in the movies.

As a young girl, I sat watching this movie thinking that I could win a golden ticket and go into this world where anything and everything was possible!

It made me realize that a river didn't need to be made out of water, but it could be made out of the most delicious, melt-in-your-mouth chocolate. You didn't really even need the golden ticket to find that river. All you needed was your own imagination. That movie was the first one that told me that I created any reality I wanted and through my own mind I could reinvent my own reality.

I also learned that anything was possible at the movies.

I was a little girl in Mexico when I figured all of this out. It was so empowering because I'll never forget walking out of the theater thinking that I could do it. I wasn't sure what I wanted to do, but I knew that it didn't matter. I could do it because Willy Wonka proved you could do it. Anyone could do it. *Even a little girl in Mexico.* I want to tell other little girls and boys that they can still do it.

That's what a good movie can do for you. It can make you think that anything is possible.

WILLY WONKA & THE CHOCOLATE FACTORY (1971). Gene Wilder, in a role recently re-created by Johnny Depp, plays an eccentric candy creator who takes a group of prize-winning children on a tour of his factory. Among the five kids is Charlie, a poor, good boy who stands out from the obnoxious others on the tour. The film's score was Oscar-nominated.

....

Oscar nominee **SALMA HAYEK** grew up in Mexico, where she spent her free time as a child in her local movie house. She shot to superstar status in her country after playing the lead on the soap opera *Teresa*. But at age twenty-four she decided to leave that behind to come to Los Angeles, where her first mission was learning English. She was cast in *Desperado* and gave what has been dubbed one of the sexiest screen stripteases in history in *From Dusk Till Dawn*. Other films include *Fools Rush In, Dogma, Wild Wild West, Traffic, Once Upon a Time in Mexico, After the Sunset,* and *Bandidas* with her friend Penelope Cruz. She received a best actress Oscar nomination for playing famed Mexican painter Frida Kahlo in *Frida*.

DIANNE HOUSTON

There is a film where Robin Williams plays a homeless man called *The Fisher King*. I love it because it takes and blends reality with dreams in an awesome, inspiring way. Isn't that why we go to the movies?

My favorite scene is in Grand Central Station where everyone is walking through and then suddenly everyone is dancing. I was in awe because my brain works that way. I want to be dancing inside all the time like they do in *The Fisher King*.

THE FISHER KING (1991). Jeff Bridges stars as a talk DJ who gives a crazy man advice that prompts a tragedy. Three years later, the guilt-ridden Bridges is saved from being burned to death by a creepy-looking Robin Williams, a street person who demands an unusual payback. In order to repay the favor, the DJ finds himself on a search for the elusive Holy Grail. Terry Gilliam directed the film that saw Mercedes Ruehl take home a best supporting actress Oscar. Williams was nominated for his lead role while other nominations went to the film's screenplay, score, and art direction.

DIANNE HOUSTON is an Oscar-nominated writer and director with various film and TV credits, including *Tuesday Morning Ride*, her Oscar-nominated short film. Her TV credits include directing *NYPD Blue*, writing *Brewster Place*, and directing *Crossing Jordan*. She recently wrote the film *Take the Lead* and wrote a big-screen biopic with hip-hop superstar Missy Elliott based on her life.

TERRENCE HOWARD

Tombstone, man. What else is as good?

Val Kilmer did it in in that movie. He just did it in! I saw it before I knew he was Val Kilmer. And it didn't matter to me if he was a star or not because he became the role. You see what I mean?

When I start any movie to this day, I watch Val play Doc Holliday in *Tombstone*. I pop it right into my DVD player. Why? Val created something I never saw in my life. He transformed himself and went back in time.

He was honest. He didn't turn away from the camera to find the character or wait half a movie to become the character. He allowed you to see the character by going to vulnerable places.

His depth showed me that possible rise as an actor.

You remember taking calculus in high school? You had to sit there busting your brain trying to figure that stuff out. You had to figure out the integral parts to get to the whole. I think of acting in this way.

I watched Val in *Tombstone* go up and down those curves to get to the role. I can navigate my own curves and integrals now as a result of watching what he did. He makes me want to challenge myself. He makes me want to do my own *Tombstone*.

And baby, if I'm home on a Saturday night, you know what I'm watching.

TOMBSTONE (1993). Val Kilmer picked up an MTV Movie Award for his lead performance as Doc Holliday in this all-star movie about Wyatt Earp (Kurt Russell), who moves to Tombstone, Arizona, to retire only to find himself in the famed shoot-out at the OK Corral.

....

The breakout star of *Hustle & Flow*, **TERRENCE HOWARD** grew up in Chicago and Cleveland and got his start in New York when he was tapped for an episode of *The Cosby Show*. Howard made his film debut in *Mr. Holland's Opus*. He had roles in *Lackawanna Blues*, *Four Brothers*, *Get Rich or Die Tryin'*, *Ray*, and *Crash* before making his Oscar-nominated turn as Djay, a pimp who wants to bust out of the urban jungle and rap, in the critically acclaimed *Hustle & Flow*.

KATE HUDSON

Are we talking guilty pleasures or really good films? Okay, a really good film. Got it!

I have to start with *The Shining*. I could probably watch it over and over again and be just as scared each time. Jack. That creepy house. Enough said.

Now, this is almost cliché, but *Casablanca* to me is . . . well, just forget it. That might be my favorite movie. I could watch that movie over and over, too. The performances are sublime. Humphrey Bogart and Ingrid Bergman are amazing together. There's that one scene where she asks Sammy the piano player to play the song. The camera just sits on her and the look on her face tells the whole story right there in one shot. It's almost like a still on her. That little moment was unbelievable to me.

I still love all of the famous lines—"Of all of the gin joints in the world, you had to come walking into mine"—all that stuff. I could recite the lines together.

You still want them to get together even if you've seen it a million times. But I love that this movie took chances. It's never as fun to have an expected ending as it is to have an unexpected ending. This movie talked about love, and in real life love can't always be. Yet, it's still heartbreaking and so bittersweet. Life is so bittersweet, and I love movies that make you feel that in your soul.

I also loved *Finding Neverland* as a more recent picture. It's another bittersweet ending, when Kate Winslet dies, but the message is that nothing in life is ever perfect. I love that message, but it's so true.

I also love *What Ever Happened to Baby Jane?* I love when she sings, "I wrote a letter to Daddy . . ." Oh forget it. Bette Davis. Please. She was an Aries, you know. And her career was so fantastic and amazing. But I think *Baby Jane* was the high point. I love that movie so much. She is just on fire. Love it, love it! I could watch it right now.

Now, we're having fun. Can we do this all day long?

••••••••••••••••••••••••••••••••••

CASABLANCA (1942). The tagline said it all: "They had a date with fate in Casablanca!" Of all of the gin joints in this world, Humphrey Bogart had to step into one in occupied Africa during World War II, where he happens to meet Ilsa Lund, played by Ingrid Bergman. It's the beginning of a beautiful, albeit much too short, romance. Line to love: "Louie, I think this is the beginning of a beautiful friendship."

WHAT EVER HAPPENED TO BABY JANE? (1962). Former child star Baby Jane Hudson, played by Bette Davis, is the caretaker from hell. Forced into serving her crippled movie star sister Blanche, expertly done with maximum stoic anguish by Joan Crawford, Jane, in the creepiest of dilapidated Hollywood mansions, performs her daily torture routines on her sis. Dialogue to love: Blanche—"You wouldn't be able to do these awful things to me if I weren't still in this chair." Jane—"But ya are, Blanche, ya are in that chair."

••••••••••••••••••••••••••••••••••

Uber cutie **KATE HUDSON** brings her own brand of California exuberance and cool to the big screen. The daughter of Goldie Hawn and her ex-husband Bill Hudson, Kate was performing for the family, including her mom, actor Kurt Russell (considered "Pa" to Kate), and her brothers from an early age. She made her film debut in *Desert Blue* and nabbed an Oscar nomination for playing rock groupie (dubbed a Band Aide) Penny Lane in Cameron Crowe's *Almost Famous*. She has also starred in *Le Divorce*; *How to Lose a Guy in 10 Days*; *Raising Helen*; *The Skeleton Key*; and *You, Me and Dupree*.

FELICITY HUFFMAN

I absolutely love *The English Patient*, but it must rank second because my favorite film of all time is *Sense and Sensibility*. I love Emma Thompson and Alan Rickman. And it's just a beautiful movie about love and longing. I can't ever forget that scene when Hugh Grant comes in and says to Emma, "I'm not married." And she loses it and cries and gasps. She can't stop crying and neither can I. It's one of the great all-time movie moments. I can't get past Alan Rickman in the film either because he has such longing for love. It's all over his face, and his eyes are just so heartbreaking. You can see his pain without him even saying a word.

SENSE AND SENSIBILITY (1995). Ang Lee directed Oscar-nominated actresses Emma Thompson (lead) and Kate Winslet (support) in an adaptation of the Jane Austen novel that also gathered nominations for best picture, cinematography, costuming, and original score. Thompson picked up her Oscar for adapting the screenplay from the classic about two sisters who are opposites in life and love. Rickman and Grant play the men who might just sweep them off their feet.

Native of Aspen, Colorado, Oscar nominee, and Desperate House-wife **FELICITY HUFFMAN**—who calls herself "Flicka"—is the youngest of seven daughters. She met husband and fellow actor William H. Macy when they worked together early in both of their careers at the Atlanta Theater Company. She starred on TV's *Sports Night* and in the films *Raising Helen* and *Christmas with the Kranks*. Huffman received a best actress Oscar nomination for playing a pre-op transgender named Bree in *Transamerica*. She also plays Lynette Scavo on the popular TV series *Desperate Housewives*.

PETER JACKSON

I was nine years old, and we had this great black-and-white TV at my parents' house in the den. One Friday night, I was really bored, so I sat down in front of the TV and saw this giant monkey hanging off the Empire State Building. I got goose bumps. About two hours later, I saw these men kill King Kong. I sat there thinking, *Why would they kill the most magnificent creature in the world? Why? Why?* I remember sitting on my shag carpeting and just crying and crying. Why would they kill something that could beat up a T. rex? This was an ape with guts, heart, and soul.

I saw the original *King Kong* in the days before the VCR. We didn't have revival houses in my neighborhood either. But I did find a way to buy a copy of the 1933 version of *King Kong* to play on a super-8 projector. I'd put up a clean white sheet on my bedroom wall and project it over and over again. The two scenes that I played over and over again were the T. rex fight and the finale at the Empire State Building. I also loved the idea of a remote, hidden island like Scull Island filled with giant apes.

Now, this is escapism at its very best. The story entirely revolves around the suspension of disbelief—and in this case, I don't want to be a believer.

The day after I saw *King Kong* for the first time, I got out my parents' stop-motion camera. I made myself a clay brontosaurus and a big gorilla and started filming using frame-by-frame animation. That [his 2005 *Kong* remake] was really just the film I tried to make at age twelve with my super-8. You could say filming that ape had been a long-standing ambition of mine.

....

KING KONG (1933) was originally billed as "The Most Awesome Thriller of All Time." Co-directed by Merian C. Cooper and Ernest B. Schoedsack, the Fay Wray classic revolves around a film crew that stumbles upon a tropical island. It's the perfect exotic backdrop until one of the very large, very hairy, very possessive locals decides he has a yen for the blonde babe Faye. The film also stars Robert Armstrong and Bruce Cabot.

....

Pukera Bay, New Zealand, wundershooter **PETER JACKSON** is one of only five directors in the history of motion pictures who has won a best picture, best director, and best screenplay Oscar during the same year for one film: in his case, *The Lord of the Rings: The Return of the King*. Jackson also directed the wildly popular *The Lord of the Rings: The Fellowship of the Ring* and *The Lord of the Rings: The Two Towers*. His other films include *Heavenly Creatures*, *The Frighteners*, and a remake of *King Kong*.

TIM JOHNSON

This is an answer that will change depending on when you ask me. It could change an hour from now. But I'm going to say three movies—*Dr. Strangelove*, *Searching for Bobby Fischer*, and *Out of the Past*, which is great film noir. I'd pack all three of them if I had to go to a desert island.

Searching for Bobby Fischer is a beautiful film about a child thrown into this world of chess, which is very cutthroat. I find it very inspiring because you really go into this little boy's world and see his pressures.

I love *Dr. Strangelove* because it was the epitome of character comedy. The first time you see it you kind of don't laugh. By the time you're on your third viewing you're laughing really hard. Things that are punch lines don't appear to be so until you really get to know this movie. As a teenager, I worked at Osco Drugstore as a stock boy. Every Thursday night, the stock boys would act out *Dr. Strangelove*. We had a couple of guys who had it memorized. I know just about every line, too, which is great fun.

As for *Out of the Past*, it's just whip-smart dialogue. It asks: Who do you trust? Plus, Robert Mitchum was the coolest human being. He was built like a door and a brilliant leading man. I also love how this movie was beautifully shot in black and white.

DR. STRANGELOVE OR: HOW I LEARNED TO STOP WORRYING AND LOVE THE BOMB (1964). Considered one of Stanley Kubrick's masterworks, this Cold War black comedy stars Peter Sellers as three men attempting to avert a nuclear disaster engineered by a mad U.S. Air Force colonel (Sterling Hayden). Sellers plays an Adlai Stevenson–

type U.S. president, a British captain, and the ex-Nazi Strangelove. It's a potent intellectual jab at the absurdity of war and the men who make it, earning Sellers, Kubrick, the film, and its screenplay Oscar nominations.

SEARCHING FOR BOBBY FISCHER (1993). Directed by Steven Zallian, the film features a boy chess genius who will only go so far in order to become a champion. Max Pomeranc plays little Josh Waitzkin flanked by Joe Mantegna and Joan Allen as his parents. Ben Kingsley is a chess champion who teaches the little boy.

OUT OF THE PAST (1947). The past of a onetime private eye returns to haunt him when a gambler he once double-crossed comes back into his life. Jacques Tourneur directed this National Film Registry drama that stars Robert Mitchum.

....

Animation director **TIM JOHNSON** grew up in suburban Chicago. He directed *Antz*, *Sinbad: Legend of the Seven Seas*, and *Over the Hedge*.

TOMMY LEE JONES

I have a bunch of movies I love. One of my favorites is *Dreams* by Akira Kurosawa. I like the geometry and the color of that film a lot. I also like how these two factors relate and are components of the narrative progression.

Another favorite film is *Bring Me the Head of Alfredo Garcia*. I like the open frames used in that motion picture. I also like the scene where there is this little pregnant girl sitting by a duck pond. It's one of the most beautiful images Sam Peckinpah ever shot. The boldness and audacity of it was impressive, and the colors were brilliant. I also enjoyed the movement. There are times when I want to turn the sound off and imagine I'm a dog looking at a mobile in the air. I want to pretend these are never-before-seen images. I love the way Peckinpah would move things and people. He had such a visual rhythm. It's a beautiful film.

I also like *Angel and the Badman*. I love the honesty of John Wayne's work. It's about water. It's about violence. It's about peace. It's about how these things might interface. I think it's the most sophisticated film the Duke ever made and I like everything the Duke ever made.

DREAMS (1990). Akira Kurosawa directed these stories based on his own dreams. It's almost like eight separate films, including "Sunshine Through the Rain," "The Peach Orchard," "The Blizzard," and "The Tunnel."

BRING ME THE HEAD OF ALFREDO GARCIA (1974). Director

Sam Peckinpah called the shots and wrote the story of a wealthy Mexican rancher facing a family scandal that forces him to utter the now-famous line, "Bring me the head of Alfredo Garcia." The plot thickens and includes bounty hunters and a piano player who try to gain access to a financial windfall. Of course, it's Peckinpah, so there's a bloody and violent end result. The film stars Gig Young, Warren Oates, Isela Vega, and Kris Kristofferson.

ANGEL AND THE BADMAN (1947). The Duke, aka John Wayne, plays Quirt Evans, a bad hombre who is nursed back to life and then is romanced by a beautiful and innocent Quaker girl played by Gail Russell. Dubbed the most romantic of Wayne's extensive film list, he's a man who has to choose between a life of crime and a life of love.

....

Texas-born **TOMMY LEE JONES** studied English literature at Harvard University, where his roommate was future Vice President Al Gore. Ten days after graduating, Jones landed his first role on Broadway in *A Patriot for Me* and then made his feature film debut in 1970 in *Love Story*. He did a slew of roles, including *Jackson County Jail*, *Eyes of Laura Mars*, *The Betsy*, and *Coal Miner's Daughter*. Jones won an Emmy for playing murderer Gary Gilmore in the TV movie *The Executioner's Song*. He followed that with another memorable TV role as cowboy Woodrow Call in the critically acclaimed CBS miniseries *Lonesome Dove*. Jones was nominated for an Oscar for playing Clay Shaw in *JFK* and won a best supporting actor Oscar in 1993 for *The Fugitive*. He has also starred in *Heaven & Earth*, *Natural Born Killers*, *Blue Sky*, *The Client*, *Cobb*, and *Batman Forever*. He made his directorial debut with *The Three Burials of Melquiades Estrada* to rave reviews.

NICOLE KIDMAN

I love Meryl Streep movies, and she deserves a lot of accolades, but if you look at Shirley MacLaine's performances over the years, you'll be in awe. Here is a woman who has been in some of the greatest comedic and dramatic movies ever. She's made us laugh and cry—especially in one of my favorite films, *Terms of Endearment*.

Why do I love it? Because you do laugh one minute and cry the next. It's hard to balance that type of role, but Shirley does it beautifully. She was literally walking a tightrope with that movie, but pulled it off. She was the heart and soul of that film as the mother. She not only dealt with her daughter's illness, but also made Jack Nicholson a better man in the movie. She held her own with Jack in those scenes where he romances her, and he's really good! What a woman! What a movie!

....

TERMS OF ENDEARMENT (1983). Call her the mother from hell or one hell of a mother, Shirley MacLaine gets both titles as a woman who checks to make sure her daughter is breathing as a little girl and then holds her own breath while her adult daughter marries a man destined to ruin her life. The film won five Academy Awards, including best picture, best director for James L. Brooks, best screenplay for Brooks, best actor for Jack Nicholson, and best actress for Shirley MacLaine, who beat out her co-star, Debra Winger, for the Oscar statue. Everyone knows the film revolves around obsessive mother Aurora Greenway (MacLaine) who clashes over the decades with her long-suffering daughter Emma (Winger). The supporting cast includes

Nicholson as the ready-for-lift-off former astronaut, plus Danny De-Vito, Jeff Daniels, and John Lithgow. Has anything ever been more heartbreaking than Aurora screaming at those nurses, "Just give my daughter the shot!"

••••••••••••••••••••••••••••••••••

Oscar winner **NICOLE KIDMAN** is a gorgeous Aussie import who made her debut in the Down Under film *Flirting*. She caught the attention of American audiences in the 1989 film *Dead Calm*. Her early roles include *Days of Thunder*, *Billy Bathgate*, *Far and Away*, and *My Life*. She rose to the A list with starring roles in movies *To Die For*, *Portrait of a Lady*, *Eyes Wide Shut*, and *The Peacemaker*. Kidman was nominated for a best actress Oscar for playing Satine in *Moulin Rouge!* She won the Oscar for playing Virginia Woolf in *The Hours*. Other films include *Birthday Girl*, *Dogville*, *The Human Stain*, *Cold Mountain*, *The Stepford Wives*, *Birth*, *The Interpreter*, and *Bewitched*.

Q' ORIANKA KILCHER

I just love *Elf*. When I'm sad, I put on *Elf* and laugh to it. It's so gorgeous and carefree. The movie always makes me smile. When Will Ferrell as Elf picks up the gum on the street in New York, it's so disgusting—and so funny. I love Will Ferrell. He's one of the funniest people. He's funny without trying to be funny. He's also such a big guy in the elf costume.

ELF (2003). Will Ferrell is the man-sized elf sent to New York City from the North Pole to find his true identity. (Hint: He was slipped into Santa's sack by mistake.) The hit secured Ferrell's leading-man status onscreen.

Q' ORIANKA KILCHER was born in Germany and grew up in Hawaii with her mother, who is an artist and musician. At age six, she picked up a tattered piece of paper in the streets, which changed her life. It was an advertisement for an acting class. At age eight, she moved with her mother and two brothers to Los Angeles to start her acting career. Commercials and TV guest appearances led to a small role in the 2000 movie *How the Grinch Stole Christmas*. She was only fourteen years old when director Terrence Malick cast her as Pocahontas to Colin Farrell's John Smith in *The New World*.

VAL KILMER

I really like *The Full Monty* and *Anchorman*. I know I'm getting really deep on you with these answers, but I like those movies and those are my answers. Maybe this is as deep as it gets in your forties!

Yes, it used to be the classics for me and now it's *Anchorman*. In fact, I did a musical last year onstage. For the first few weeks during the down times I was running around backstage doing dumb Will Ferrell jokes because he plays this great pompous dumb guy in *Anchorman*. No one backstage knew what I was even talking about. I like this movie so much that I got a copy of the film and ran it so my fifty-five cast-mates could understand it.

THE FULL MONTY (1997). Six unemployed British steelworkers find an unusual way to raise money the old-fashioned way—by stripping—in this Oscar-nominated comedy. The film won an Academy Award for its musical score, but lost in the categories of director (Peter Cattaneo), original screenplay, and film. The movie was turned into a Broadway play and proved a springboard for actor Mark Addy, who went on to American television and films.

ANCHORMAN: THE LEGEND OF RON BURGUNDY (2004). No Oscars for this low-key parody of the world of male-dominated television news, but Ben Stiller, in a cameo, did score a Razzie for worst actor thanks to his role in this, *Along Came Polly*, *Dodgeball*, and *Starsky & Hutch*. Star Will Ferrell didn't fare as well at the box office despite loads of inside laughs for a comedy about a San Diego newsman forced to adjust to a new female employee (Christina Applegate) who arrives at his TV station in this '70s-set film. *The 40 Year Old Virgin* star Steve Carell makes his mark in a supporting role.

....

Los Angeles native **VAL KILMER** studied at Juilliard and began his career acting on stage. He made his film debut in *Top Secret!* playing rocker Nick Rivers. He was Tom Cruise's foil, Iceman, in *Top Gun* and played Jim Morrison for Oliver Stone in *The Doors*. Kilmer played icons Elvis Presley in *True Romance* and Doc Holliday in *Tombstone*. Other roles include *Batman Forever, Heat, The Island of Dr. Moreau, The Ghost and the Darkness, The Saint, Alexander, Kiss Kiss Bang Bang,* and *Déjà Vu*.

CHRIS KLEIN

I have a childhood love of the movies. I grew up enamored by going to a theater and sitting in the dark. For sentimental reasons, I love *The Jungle Book*. I remember being a little boy when my mother took me to see *The Jungle Book* for the first time. I wanted to hang out with Mowgli and dance with Baloo. I wanted to hang out with that bear. I remember thinking as a little boy if I believed it hard enough then I could jump into that movie screen and live it.

I also love *Harvey* with Jimmy Stewart. I love that one because of Stewart's simplicity. When you watch that movie, you actually believe Harvey exists. You want to meet a big six-foot white rabbit. I have wonderful memories of watching that movie with my grandfather, who could recite every single line of it. I fell in love with the film because of my grandfather's enthusiasm. He loved it and I will love it forever.

THE JUNGLE BOOK (1967). Based on the novel by Rudyard Kipling, it's the ultimate animated jungle tale of Bagheera the Panther and Baloo the Bear. Together with their other 'toon animal friends they must coax a little boy to ditch fun jungle life to reunite with the humans in civilization. But why would the boy want to leave when the tagline for the film says it all: "The Jungle Is Jumpin'!"

HARVEY (1950). James Stewart won an Oscar nomination for his role as a drunk who has an unseen friend he calls Harvey. Harvey is a six-feet-three-and-a-half-inches-tall rabbit that no one but Elwood P. Dowd (Stewart) can see, although Elwood's sister (Josephine Hull, who won a best supporting actress Oscar for the role) can see him at times. Sis winds up in a sanatorium by mistake before the doctor in charge goes after Elwood.

....

Illinois native **CHRIS KLEIN** was discovered walking the halls of his high school by director Alexander Payne, who was casting what became the indie hit *Election*. He played the stupid but sweet football player. He went on to play Chris "Oz" Ostreicher in *American Pie*. Klein also starred in *Here on Earth, Say It Isn't So, American Pie 2, Rollerball, We Were Soldiers, The United States of Leland, Just Friends*, and *American Dreamz*.

QUEEN LATIFAH

I got a couple of favorite films. I do love *Claudine* and *Taps* as two of my favorites. First of all, both of them had kids, and I love movies with kids. Specifically, *Claudine* starred Diahann Carroll, and she always reminded me of my mom. She was a well-spoken *sista* in the 'hood—and that was my mom. My mom was well spoken, and like Claudine, she didn't have a lot of money but tried to do the best she could with some style and some flair and some class in the ghetto. I swear my mom could have played that role.

I love *Taps* because it's a film with all these kids who were empowered. It reminded me of *Lord of the Flies*, which was also one of my favorite movies. Both are sad and tragic, but I saw them as a kid, and it was powerful for me to watch other kids who tried to take control of their destinies—right or wrong. They still tried to take charge and change things.

Now would I be wrong if I added *Blacula* to the list? It's one of my favorite movies! I am who I am because of *Blacula*! Just kidding about that last part, but it's a great movie because it's so cheesy and scary! As a kid, I watched that movie on the end of my seat. Even the makeup scared me. And I'll never forget this one scene where they had a nurse who had been killed. No one closed the door. And this guy is walking around the morgue singing, and someone comes running out of one those little side rooms in the morgue where the nurse's body was stashed. The girl was screaming and running. Scared the hell out of me!

· ·

CLAUDINE (1974). Diahann Carroll won an Academy Award nomination for her role as the Harlem mother of six who's on welfare when she falls for a garbage man (James Earl Jones).

TAPS (1981). Yes, that's a very young, totally intense, slightly overweight Tom Cruise playing a cadet in Harold Becker's drama about a venerable military academy that's about to be demolished to make way for new housing. With a by-the-rules commander (George C. Scott), the young cadets (led by Timothy Hutton) decide to take matters into their own hands by facing off against construction workers and, ultimately, real-life military. A young Sean Penn also is featured.

BLACULA (1972). You must love a movie that has the tagline: "Rising from the Echoing Corridors of Hell, an Awesome Being of the Supernatural—With Satanic Power of Sheer Dread. Chained Forever to a Slavery More Vile Than Any Before Endured!" The plot—yes, there is one—involves two antique collectors who happen to purchase the coffin where the body of an African prince named Mamuwalde (William Marshall), bitten by Dracula many centuries ago, is waiting to come back from the dead. Luckily, he returns to Los Angeles, where he begins a bloodthirsty quest. It even spawned the sequel *Scream Blacula Scream* the following year.

· ·

Her real name is Dana Owens, but this little girl from East Orange, New Jersey, was always a queen. In fact, **QUEEN LATIFAH** changed her name after reading that Latifah means "sensitive and delicate" in Arabic. The Queen grew up in families of cops, but instead defected from the family business to become a top hip-hop artist. After a stint on TV's *Living Single*, she began her film career with *Jungle Fever*, *Juice*, *Set It Off*, *The Bone Collector*, and *Brown Sugar*. She received an Oscar nomination for playing Matron Mama Morton in the Oscar-winning movie musical *Chicago* and had a huge box office hit with *Bringing Down the House*.

SANAA LATHAN

I love *Wuthering Heights*. It's just so incredibly romantic. That movie makes me cry each and every time, because it's the ultimate tortured love story. Oh my God, I can just see their faces in that film, and I want to cry for those lovers.

I love all the old movies, but another favorite is *Woman of the Year* with Katharine Hepburn. She's such an amazing talent, and I can't take my eyes off of her. I also love the old Doris Day movies like *Pillow Talk*. It's just one of those great mindless movies. This might sound strange, but I love Technicolor. It just keeps you cheerful. Those movies reflect a Hollywood where everything is lollipops and roses. Of course, there are no black people in these movies, or they just played the maid.

Doris was amazing on the big screen. I loved everything about her, from her smooth voice to her A-line skirts. Again, just looking at her navigate life made you feel good. She was so spunky and strong during a time when many women were quiet. But in movies like *Pillow Talk*, Doris was in control. She was a little diva in the most delicious way, but no one knew it.

WUTHERING HEIGHTS (1939). "I am Heathcliff!" Merle Oberon screamed, issuing a battle cry for all lovers obsessed. The object of her desire, the wild, tortured boy brought home by a Yorkshire farmer to live among his family, is played by Laurence Olivier, who was Oscar-nominated for his lead performance. The romantic film set in the English moors was nominated for best picture, director (William Wyler), music, supporting actress (Geraldine Fitzgerald), art direction, and screenplay, but won only for its moody black-and-white cinematography.

WOMAN OF THE YEAR (1942). This classic pairing of real-life lovers Katharine Hepburn and Spencer Tracy has them starting out as newspaper reporters who don't like each other. They eventually fall in love, get married, and then hit a snag when Hepburn's feminist ways intrude. It's a comedy with contemporary applications that won Hepburn an Oscar nomination and its screenplay the golden statuette.

PILLOW TALK (1959). Rock Hudson and Doris Day were perfect onscreen lovers, as witnessed in this romantic comedy about a man and woman who hate each other but share a telephone line. He decides to woo her by disguising his voice and romance ensues. The movie won an Oscar for its original screenplay but lost out in the categories of best actress (Day), supporting actress (Thelma Ritter), art direction, and music.

....

Pronounced *Sa-NAA*, **SANAA LATHAN**'s name in Swahili means "work of art." This screen beauty grew up in New York City and studied acting at Yale School of Drama, where she frequently appeared in stage productions. Off-Broadway productions led to film roles in *Blade*, *Life*, *The Wood*, *The Best Man*, *Love & Basketball*, *Disappearing Acts*, *Brown Sugar*, *Out of Time*, the sci-fi classic *AVP: Alien vs. Predator*, and *Something New*. She was nominated for a Tony in 2004 for her performance as Beneatha in the revival of *A Raisin in the Sun*.

CLORIS LEACHMAN

I'm going to pick *To Each His Own* as my all-time-favorite film. It's just so gloriously soapy. Olivia de Havilland is a small-town girl in World War I who has an illegitimate son with a pilot. You got lust!

She gives the boy up to her sister to raise. You got pain!

As if that's not bad enough, cut to years later during World War II when Olivia is in England and sees her now-grown son who is, incidentally, drop-dead gorgeous. You got angst!

I could die all over again just talking about this movie and remembering that moment when she sees her son. She even helps her boy arrange a wedding at the top of this hotel. She pretends to be "a friend." All of this time, Olivia's sister is still pretending to be this young man's mother. But then he realizes that something is terribly, terribly wrong. He just feels it. And he walks over to Olivia at the wedding. The band swells, and the young man says, "I believe this is our dance . . . Mother!"

Just kill me now!

TO EACH HIS OWN (1946). Olivia de Havilland won her best actress Oscar playing an unwed mother who gives up her child in World War I and spends the rest of her life loving the boy from afar. It's a first-caliber tearjerker whose screenplay won an Oscar nomination.

CLORIS LEACHMAN has won five Emmys for her work on television. She began her career with *The Ford Theatre Hour*, *The Actor's Studio*, *General Electric Theater*, and *The Philco Television Playhouse*. She did early TV roles on classic series, including *Wagon Train*, *77 Sunset Strip*, *Kiss Me Deadly*, *Dr. Kildare*, *Perry Mason*, and *The Virginian*. She also played Phyllis Lindstrom on *The Mary Tyler Moore Show* and her own series *Phyllis*. Her films include *Butch Cassidy and the Sundance Kid*, *Lovers and Other Strangers*, *High Anxiety*, *The Muppet Movie*, *History of the World: Part 1*, and *Texasville*. Leachman won a best supporting actress Oscar for her role as Ruth Popper in *The Last Picture Show*.

HEATH LEDGER

I have to say *The Wizard of Oz*. I saw it about ten times when I was little, because it was the only film my parents allowed me to see as a kid. I just love the magic of it.

THE WIZARD OF OZ (1939). Though it didn't win the biggest award on Oscar night, it was nominated for best picture and managed to snag statuettes for its original score and original song, "Over the Rainbow." No one else in the beloved musical—not Judy Garland as Dorothy, the girl from Kansas; not Bert Lahr as the Cowardly Lion; not Ray Bolger as the Scarecrow; and not Jack Haley as the Tin Man—was nominated. The film airs regularly on television as new generations respond to the fantasy tale of a girl spun into the air along with her dog, Toto, and deposited in the Land of Oz. If she wants to get home, she has to "follow the yellow brick road" and go "off to see the Wizard."

HEATH LEDGER was nominated for his role as a loving cowboy in the recent critically acclaimed hit *Brokeback Mountain*. He grew up in Perth, Australia, and came to America as a young man with an acting dream. His first role was in the horror film *Two Hands*, which he followed with the teen hit *10 Things I Hate About You*. He played Mel Gibson's oldest son in *The Patriot*. Other productions include *Casanova*, *Monster's Ball*, *Ned Kelly*, *The Order*, *The Four Feathers*, and *A Knight's Tale*.

JOHN LEGUIZAMO

I'd have to say *Annie Hall* is one of my favorite movies of all time. I know it sounds like an odd choice, but I love this film, because it's really funny. It was also edgy and took so many risks. This wasn't a conventional romantic comedy. And I love the fact that they don't stay together in the end. You didn't see that much in movies when *Annie Hall* came out. Life isn't just about happy endings. That makes *Annie Hall* so brilliant and unique.

I gotta say *Mean Streets* too. Hey, I'm a guy. It was such an urban, real experience. De Niro was so phenomenal in it. I had never seen acting like that in my life. I saw *Mean Streets* when I was twenty-one. My jaw was hitting the ground—especially because I was sitting in a New York theater watching this gritty story. I looked at De Niro up there and I was like, *That's what I want to do*. I love that so many movies came from *Mean Streets*. It was an inspiration to so many people.

Later on I bought *Mean Streets* in every form. I have it on cassette tape, laser disc, and now on DVD. Any form it comes out on, I rebuy it.

ANNIE HALL (1977). "La-dee-dah" entered cinema lexicon when star Diane Keaton said it in Woody Allen's Oscar-winning film. Director Allen and his leading lady also picked up Academy Awards for the quirky romantic comedy about a New York comedian with as many hang-ups as his girlfriend has. Allen and Marshall Brickman took home screenwriting honors as well for the film that became a fashion trendsetter, thanks to Keaton's baggy pants and vests.

MEAN STREETS (1973). Martin Scorsese is at his very best in his own New York 'hood. The auteur directed the tale of a small-time hustler named John "Johnny Boy" Civello (Robert De Niro) who must survive life and not get taken out by the other punks on the very mean streets of Little Italy. Harvey Keitel plays Charlie Cappa, a man torn between the staid life of his uncle and the cutting-edge ways of Johnny Boy. An easy choice? Fugghettaboutit.

....

Mouth-blazing, fast-talking comic-turned-actor **JOHN LEGUIZAMO** was born in Bogotá, Colombia, and at age four moved to Queens, New York, with his family. He studied at New York University and then broke into the movies with roles in *Casualties of War, Die Hard 2, Hangin' with the Homeboys, Regarding Henry, Out for Justice, Carlito's Way,* and *A Pyromaniac's Love Story.* He received critical acclaim for *To Wong Foo Thanks for Everything, Julie Newmar.* He has also starred in *Executive Decision, The Fan, Romeo + Juliet, The Pest, Spawn, Summer of Sam, Moulin Rouge!, Assault on Precinct 13, The Honeymooners,* and *Where God Left His Shoes.* He plays Dr. Victor Clemente on the hit series *ER.* Leguizamo also voices Sid the Sloth in *Ice Age* and *Ice Age 2: The Meltdown.*

TÉA LEONI

I love James L. Brooks's *Terms of Endearment*. There is no winking. There was an absolute sincerity from these performers. Shirley MacLaine is so real. When the movie opens and she's worried that her baby is not breathing, she shakes the baby. You hear a sigh of relief from her when she feels the baby breathe. You see that sigh of relief on Shirley's face and then feel the joy of her footsteps as a parent going back to her own bedroom knowing that her child is still alive. It's just such a true emotion.

Every moment that follows is as real, even later, when her child is truly dying, which are some of the most heartbreaking moments I've ever seen on film. That makes it a genius film to me.

TERMS OF ENDEARMENT (1983). Call her the mother from hell or one hell of a mother, Shirley MacLaine gets both titles as a woman who checks to make sure her daughter is breathing as a little girl and then holds her own breath while her adult daughter marries a man destined to ruin her life. The film won five Academy Awards, including best picture, best director for James L. Brooks, best screenplay for Brooks, best actor for Jack Nicholson, and best actress for Shirley MacLaine, who beat out her co-star, Debra Winger, for the Oscar statue. Everyone knows the film revolves around obsessive mother Aurora Greenway (MacLaine) who clashes over the decades with her long-suffering daughter Emma (Winger). The supporting cast includes Nicholson as the ready-for-lift-off former astronaut, plus Danny DeVito, Jeff Daniels, and John Lithgow. Has anything ever been more heartbreaking than Aurora screaming at those nurses, "Just give my daughter the shot!"

....

Comic actress **TÉA LEONI** began her big-screen career with bases loaded in Penny Marshall's A *League of Their Own*. She starred in the TV series *Flying Blind* and *The Naked Truth*. Her movie credits include *Bad Boys, Flirting with Disaster, Deep Impact, The Family Man, Jurassic Park III, Spanglish*, and *Fun with Dick and Jane*. Her husband, David Duchovny, directed her in the drama *House of D*.

EUGENE LEVY

I know a lot of men will say *Lawrence of Arabia*. I love the desert as much as the next guy. But it's not my favorite film.

The best film ever made is *Godfather II*. It's a remarkable movie with great performances, a great storyline, and a great cast. Both *Godfathers* are up there for me. But the second one is one of those rare sequels that actually surpassed the original. It's also visually stunning.

I love the part when they go down to Cuba. It was so exciting. I loved what Lee Strasberg brought to this movie. It was just an amazing performance. I watched Pacino but I studied Strasberg. Watching the two work in a scene, it was like the student and the teacher. Fascinating. It's one of those movies you can watch over and over. It's remarkable.

THE GODFATHER: PART II (1974). Considered by many the best sequel in film history, Francis Ford Coppola's middle movie in the Mario Puzo novel–based trilogy continues the saga of Mafia boss Michael Corleone (Al Pacino) while telling in flashback the story of his father's rise to power in New York's Little Italy. Robert De Niro plays the young Vito Corleone in the Italian language and won a best supporting actor Oscar for his performance. Pacino didn't win for his best actor nomination. Neither did Michael V. Gazzo, Lee Strasberg (supporting actors), Talia Shire (supporting actress), or Theadora Van Runkle (costumer). But the sweeping saga of an Italian family was crowned with Oscars for best picture, art direction, director (Coppola), music, and adapted screenplay.

....

Known for his thick brows and high and lowbrow humor, **EUGENE LEVY** was part of the original cast on the legendary *Second City TV*. Hailing from Ontario, Canada, Levy has an eclectic filmography, including *Vacation*, *Splash*, *Waiting for Guffman*, and *American Pie*, in which he played the unnamed character of Jim's Dad. He has also starred in *Best in Show*, *The Ladies Man*, *Down to Earth*, *American Pie 2*, *Bringing Down the House*, *A Mighty Wind*, *American Wedding*, *New York Minute*, *The Man*, *Cheaper By the Dozen 2*, and *For Your Consideration*.

JET LI

Star Wars, the very first one. I loved it. Let me please explain it to you. The special effects were great. But since I am a Buddhist, I must say more about this film. As much as I liked the ship, I liked the message of the power of the Force. I like how George Lucas says that the Force is within you. Very Buddhist thinking. We need more messages like that in big movies. Oh, and more spaceships is good too.

STAR WARS (1977). Writer-director George Lucas launched his career and the whole *Star Wars* merchandising empire with this vehicle. It won Oscars for art direction, costumes, visual effects, editing, original score, and sound, but lost its bids for best picture, director, supporting actor (Alec Guinness), music, and other technical categories. It became the first of six *Star Wars* movies that told the tale of Luke Skywalker; his sister, Princess Leia; and the evil Darth Vader, whose true identity was to come much later. When Lucas began releasing three prequels to the *Star Wars* saga, he renamed the original film *Star Wars: Episode IV—A New Hope*, and it actually became the fourth in the new order. Starring Mark Hamill as Skywalker, the adventure introduced a self-assured Harrison Ford in the role of Han Solo, a dashing love interest for Leia.

....

Asian action icon **JET LI** grew up in Beijing, China, where he started studying the martial art of wushu at age eight and later won five gold medals at the Chinese championships. After starring in a slew of Asian films, he has appeared in the American films *Lethal Weapon 4*, *Romeo Must Die*, *Kiss of the Dragon*, *The One*, and *Cradle 2 the Grave*. He's the second-biggest Asian action star after Jackie Chan.

DELROY LINDO

I love *Children of Paradise*. I love that one because of what it says about the human condition and love. It's a beautiful film.

I love *"Breaker" Morant*. The scene that comes to my mind every-time I think about this favorite film is when Edward Woodward and Bryan Brown are walking up a hill to their execution. Edward takes his hand. They hold hands! I remember the first time I saw the film and then came this moment. I just bawled like a baby!

I saw it back in the days of the 1980s. I sat through it twice to see that moment again. I cried the second time. The coming together of human beings. These guys are about to die. One human being to another, they reach out and they're connecting. It's human beings reaching out to each other, so we can all live and survive and be human.

I also love *Sugar Cane Alley*. I love the grandmother and what she does to make sure that her grandchild goes to school. It's just the way that she is so determined. Nothing is going to stop this child from go-ing to school.

The larger point that unites all these films has to do with the hu-man condition and what we all do to have a life. Good films affirm our lives.

CHILDREN OF PARADISE (1945). This Marcel Carné tragedy stars Arletty and Jean-Louis Barrault as would-be lovers, separated by time and circumstance, who eventually find each other and experience the love they've always wanted to share. Unfortunately, there are others in

their lives and jealousy has its consequences. The French film is considered a classic.

"BREAKER" MORANT (1980). The tagline says it all: "When they
speak of heroes—of villains—of men who look for action, who choose
between honor and revenge—they tell the story of Breaker Morant."
The film revolves around three Aussie lieutenants who are court-
martialed for killing prisoners. Bruce Beresford directs Edward Woodward and Bryan Brown.

SUGARCANE ALLEY (1983). Euzhan Palcy directed this story set
in Martinique in the 1930s about a poor boy named José and his
grandfather, who live in a sugarcane-cutting village. José knows his
way out is studying and getting a scholarship.

....

Powerful **DELROY LINDO** was raised in England and Canada. He
graduated from the American Conservatory Theater in San Francisco
and then made his film debut as the army sergeant in *More American
Graffiti*. He has done roles on Broadway and in movies, including
Malcolm X, *Crooklyn*, *Clockers*, *Get Shorty*, *Broken Arrow*, *Feeling
Minnesota*, *Ransom*, *The Cider House Rules*, *Romeo Must Die*, *Gone
in Sixty Seconds*, *The Core*, *Lackawanna Blues*, *Sahara*, and *Domino*.

LINDSAY LOHAN

I love everything about Ann-Margret. *Kitten with a Whip* is one of my favorite movies. And I also love *Bye Bye Birdie*. Ann was just so much fun and she was wild. You couldn't stop her. She was incredible. Sexy. Amazing.

I also loved *Niagara*. It's a beautiful film, and Marilyn Monroe is one of my favorites. You just can't stop watching her. Can I add *Pretty Woman* and *The Silence of the Lambs* to the list? Now I've covered every genre.

KITTEN WITH A WHIP (1964). If you want to know what made men swoon over red-haired Ann-Margret, this is the thriller to see. In a midriff top and tight slacks, she plays a delinquent who kidnaps a politician after setting her detention center on fire. It's a morality tale that doesn't really get moral until the principals arrive in Tijuana.

BYE BYE BIRDIE (1963). At the height of his popularity, crooner Bobby Rydell took on a lead role opposite Ann-Margret in a musical about a rock star who travels to a small Ohio town to make his farewell TV appearance before joining the army. Jesse Pearson played the rocker Conrad Birdie, an Elvis-like phenomenon scheduled to sing on *The Ed Sullivan Show*. Complications arise when the rocker's songwriter (Dick Van Dyke) is plagued by his overprotective mother (Maureen Stapleton), who follows him to the Midwest. Oscar-wise, the film was nominated for best music and sound.

Young redheaded screen siren **LINDSAY LOHAN** has been dubbed "a modern-day Ann-Margret." She was born Lindsay Morgan Lohan and grew up in New York. She began her career at age three as a Ford model and eventually had more than sixty commercials on her résumé, including appearances for Wendy's, Jell-O, The Gap, and Pizza Hut. In 1996 she became little Ali Fowler on the daytime sudser *Another World*. Lohan beat out several young actresses to play the twin sisters in the remake of *The Parent Trap*. She has starred in *Freaky Friday*, *Confessions of a Teenage Drama Queen*, *Mean Girls*, *Herbie: Fully Loaded*, *A Prairie Home Companion*, *Just My Luck*, and *Bobby*.

MICHAEL LONDON

I have always loved the great Robert Mitchum movie *Out of the Past*. I love that one because I really like flawed characters. It's also a noir. He's a romantic leading man, but he's done bad things. I love that because you never want characters to be perfect. He's real and has shortcomings just the way people do in real life.

Film noir is tough to get right. This character has a lot of problems and they show them—warts and all. I love when a movie looks at humanity through a realistic lens.

OUT OF THE PAST (1947). The past of a onetime private eye returns to haunt him when a gambler he once double-crossed comes back into his life. Jacques Tourneur directed this National Film Registry drama that stars Robert Mitchum.

MICHAEL LONDON is the acclaimed producer of such films as *Sideways, House of Sand and Fog, The Guru, The Family Stone,* and *The Illusionist.*

JENNIFER LOPEZ

I grew up in the Bronx, and as a little girl I ran around telling people that I wanted to be an actress and a dancer. But I'd go home crying when people said that little Hispanic girls needed to forget about these stupid Hollywood dreams and think about a real job. I could almost believe the people who told me I was crazy to think I could make it in show business. And then I saw *West Side Story*.

I sat in that dark theater crying because here was my proof that my people could sing, dance, and act. Someone gave Rita Moreno a chance, so why couldn't I get that chance? I saw the movie about a million times on the big screen—and especially when I felt sad about my life. Each time I walked out of the theater, my own dreams were reenergized. My faith was restored.

WEST SIDE STORY (1961). In a near-sweep of the Oscars, this musical updating of *Romeo and Juliet* won awards for best picture, best direction (Robert Wise and Jerome Robbins), best supporting actor (George Chakiris), best supporting actress (Rita Moreno), best costumes, best score, best cinematography, best art direction, best editing, and best sound. The story of Tony and Maria—lovers caught between the battling street gangs called the Sharks and the Jets—lost only in the category of adapted screenplay. Starring Natalie Wood (who didn't do her own singing) and Richard Beymer, it was the first film ever to win an Oscar for two directors.

Latin triple-threat **JENNIFER LOPEZ** is a singer, actress, and businesswoman. The Bronx native got her start as a Fly Girl on the TV series *In Living Color*. The multitalented singer-dancer-actress moved on to the big screen to take on supporting roles in *My Family*, *Money Train*, *Jack*, and *Blood and Wine*. She earned raves playing the slain superstar in *Selena*. Lopez has also starred in *U Turn*, *Out of Sight*, *The Wedding Planner*, *Enough*, *Maid in Manhattan*, *Shall We Dance*, *Monster-in-Law*, *An Unfinished Life*, and *Bordertown*. She is also a platinum-selling recording artist.

JENA MALONE

I love the film *Labyrinth*. It has sentimental value to me because I saw it when I was a little kid. I'm not even kidding you when I say that I knew every single word of this movie as a child.

Why did it get to me so much? Well, first you had David Bowie, who is just about one of the coolest human beings on earth. And then there is the story, which is about searching for something. I guess I just identified with that theme.

I love this movie because I have so many childhood memories attached to going home and watching *Labyrinth* again and again. Did I mention that David Bowie is just about the coolest human being on earth?

LABYRINTH (1986). The late Muppet master Jim Henson directs the fantasy about a girl (Jennifer Connelly) who has sixteen hours to rescue her baby brother from evil Jareth, the Goblin King (David Bowie, aka The Coolest Human Being on Earth).

Serious young actress **JENA MALONE** made her small-screen debut as a little girl on Santa's lap in an episode of *Roseanne*. She received raves playing an abused girl named Ruth Anne in *Bastard Out of Carolina*, directed by Anjelica Huston. She has also starred in *Contact*, *Stepmom*, *Donnie Darko*, *The Dangerous Lives of Altar Boys*, *The United States of Leland*, *Cold Mountain*, *Saved!*, *Pride & Prejudice*, and *Lying*.

GARRY MARSHALL

Oh, I have so many favorites. But one of my all-time-favorite movies is *The Pride of the Yankees*. I'll just sit there and cry my eyes out! Lou Gehrig was just so amazing, and Gary Cooper played him just perfectly.

I also love *The Magnificent Seven*. I love those characters. Each one of them makes it work. I was just so intrigued with that film. I'm from the character school. Mork worked as a character and so did Fonzie. Same thing for the characters here in this brilliant film that I could watch again and again. I also love how the story is told here and how it unfolds. The audience gets it. When they recruited the guys, I really got into it. That was the best part of the film.

The kids are finding another one of my favorites, *The Ox-Bow Incident*. That was a Western, but it got into the internal workings of the characters. It was Henry Fonda at his best. It was like a regular story, but then there was the dilemma. Should you hang a guy? There were all these issues in the middle of a regular Western. You had the horse and the gun. All those movies look the same, but this one was different.

THE PRIDE OF THE YANKEES (1942). Gary Cooper embodied baseball star Lou Gehrig, who ended his career when he developed ALS, the nerve disease that is now referred to as Lou Gehrig's disease. The moving film chronicles Gehrig's life from childhood to his dramatic "I'm the luckiest man in the world" speech given in 1939 when he bid his farewell to baseball. Yankee great Babe Ruth played himself in the film that won an Oscar for its editing but lost in the categories of best picture, actor (Cooper), actress (Teresa Wright), art direction, story, screenplay, cinematography, sound, music, and special effects. It still ranks as one of the greatest sports movies of all time.

THE MAGNIFICENT SEVEN (1960). The story is the same as Akira Kurosawa's *The Seven Samurai*, but the setting for this John Sturges version has been changed to a small Mexican village. Seven gunfighters hired by the villagers have to confront more than one hundred bandits who are about to converge on the town. Elmer Bernstein's score was Oscar nominated, and the impressive cast includes Yul Brynner, Charles Bronson, and Steve McQueen.

THE OX-BOW INCIDENT (1943). Nominated for best picture, William A. Wellman's drama pits two drifters and some angry townspeople against a trio of men who may have murdered a farmer for his cattle. The quest for justice turns out to be anything but that in this classic Western starring Henry Fonda, Dana Andrews, and Anthony Quinn.

....

Northwestern University alum **GARRY MARSHALL** began his career writing for television, including the classic series *Make Room for Daddy*, *The Dick Van Dyke Show*, and *The Lucy Show*, and directing episodic TV, including *The Odd Couple*, *Happy Days*, *Laverne & Shirley*, and *Mork & Mindy*. He wrote jokes for *The Tonight Show* when Jack Paar sat in the host's chair. He has directed the films *Pretty Woman*, *The Princess Diaries*, *Runaway Bride*, *Frankie and Johnny*, *Beaches*, *Nothing in Common*, *Raising Helen*, *The Flamingo Kid*, and *Overboard*. He's the brother of director-actress Penny Marshall.

ROB MARSHALL

I grew up loving movie musicals. They inspired me to make movies. Let's start with a few favorites, including *Singin' in the Rain*, *Meet Me in St. Louis*, and *Funny Face*. *Funny Face* might be my favorite because it's a perfectly crafted and constructed musical. It's funny, sad, and beautiful—and the songs were constructed specifically for the film. It tells a story through dancing and singing without skipping a beat. There is not a misstep in the entire film because the characters literally come to life.

SINGIN' IN THE RAIN (1952). This famed Gene Kelly, Debbie Reynolds, and Donald O'Connor musical-comedy is considered one of Hollywood's all-time greats. Directed by Stanley Donen and Kelly, its famous splashing-in-the-rain sequence is an iconic cinema image that any movie buff recognizes on sight. Nominated for its score and supporting actress (Jean Hagen), the musical focuses on the romantic lives of Kelly and Reynolds, who play performers both trying to make the transition to "talkies."

MEET ME IN ST. LOUIS (1944). Judy Garland sings her heart out as one of four daughters of a man who has to move his family to New York from St. Louis. When she sings to her younger sister (Margaret O'Brien) that she'll be "home for Christmas, if only in my dreams," there's hardly a dry eye in the house. The film is on the National Film Registry and was nominated for Academy Awards in the categories of cinematography, song ("The Trolley Song"), score, and screenplay.

FUNNY FACE (1957). Nominated for its art direction, cinematography, costuming, and original screenplay in the Oscar race, it still wins the hearts of anyone romantic enough to embrace its story of a mousy clerk (Audrey Hepburn, trying to look drab) who captures the imagination of a famed—and much older—photographer (Fred Astaire.) Astaire's character was based on real-life photographer Richard Avedon, and the film is best remembered for its timeless Paris setting, Givenchy fashions, and memorable soundtrack, including the title song.

•••••••••••••••••••••••••••••••••

Mixing movies and music is what **ROB MARSHALL** loves to do. And if he wins an Oscar along the way for films like *Chicago*, well, that's enough to make him kick up his own heels. Marshall directed the Oscar-winning best picture *Chicago*, starring Catherine Zeta-Jones and Renée Zellweger. He also called the shots for *Memoirs of a Geisha* and TV's acclaimed *Annie*. He was nominated for six Tony Awards for shows that include *Kiss of the Spider Woman—The Musical* and *Damn Yankees!*

JESSE L. MARTIN

To Kill a Mockingbird is the best movie ever made. Are you kidding me? What's not to love? It's a beautifully acted story, including the children. It's one of the few pieces of literature that transferred to film. That's just as amazing.

It's a simply told story with no fireworks. There are a few loud moments in the movie; still you're absolutely engrossed in it. Robert Duvall plays Boo Radley. I love when he walks the little girl Scout home at the end after her brother Jim is attacked. They hold hands and he walks her home. It's just so gorgeous. It's a moment you will never forget because it's pure.

I also love *The Shawshank Redemption*. It doesn't matter when it's on and what time it's on. That ending! You can't help but cry at the end. Morgan Freeman is the premiere actor as far as I'm concerned. When he's on the bus at the end and makes the trip to see his friend Andy, my eyes well with tears. He says, "I hope the Pacific is as blue as it is in my dreams . . . I hope my friend is well . . ." It's a beautiful movie moment. Another part that gets me is when Morgan is on the ladder at the end. He's a free man and you think he can't take it, so he's going to hang himself in his hotel room like other prisoners who get out of jail and can't take freedom. But he just climbs the ladder and writes, "Red was here." He writes his name.

I'm crying at that point. I'm also thinking, *If you want someone to tell you a great story, get Morgan Freeman, and your story will be heard.* He's heartbreaking. Just look at his face. He's the king of gravitas. Everything he says has meaning.

Morgan has an amazing amount of talent and experience and knows how to use it.

....

TO KILL A MOCKINGBIRD (1962). Harper Lee's Pulitzer Prize–winning book about an Alabama lawyer who defends an innocent black man charged with raping a white woman translated into an Oscar-nominated film for which Gregory Peck won a best actor Academy Award. The film also won Oscars for art direction and adapted screenplay (Horton Foote) while receiving nominations for supporting actress (Mary Badham), cinematography, score (Elmer Bernstein), and director (Robert Mulligan).

THE SHAWSHANK REDEMPTION (1994). Considered a surprising best picture Oscar contender, this perennial favorite, based on Stephen King's novella *Rita Hayworth and the Shawshank Redemption*, stars Tim Robbins as an innocent man condemned to life in prison for the murder of his wife. Befriending an aged con (Morgan Freeman), he uses his incarceration to plan for a future outside the prison, with a special surprise reserved for the cruel warden whose taxes he has done for years. The film's seven nominations include those for the film, best actor (Freeman), cinematography, editing, music, sound, and adapted screenplay.

....

Singer-dancer-actor **JESSIE L. MARTIN** grew up in Buffalo, New York, where as a fourth-grader he was bitten by the acting bug during a school play. His big break was being cast in Jonathan Larson's Pulitzer Prize–winning Broadway musical *Rent*, and Martin recently reprised the role for the film version of the hit show. Martin has also starred on the small screen in *Ally McBeal* as Ally's lover Dr. Greg Butters, and on the popular *Law & Order* as Detective Ed Green.

RACHEL McADAMS

I really love *Willy Wonka & the Chocolate Factory*. It's so weird and such a creepy movie. Veruca is my favorite little-girl character. She's awesomely horrible to the maximum. I mean, she so inspired me in terms of playing those mean girls in *Mean Girls*. She's such a template because she's delicious.

And you can't help but wish you won a golden ticket to that chocolate factory . . . wait, maybe you wish that you didn't win one!

WILLY WONKA & THE CHOCOLATE FACTORY (1971). Gene Wilder, in a role recently re-created by Johnny Depp, plays an eccentric candy creator who takes a group of prize-winning children on a tour of his factory. Among the five kids is Charlie, a poor, good boy who stands out from the obnoxious others on the tour. The film's score was Oscar-nominated.

Gorgeous screen newcomer **RACHEL McADAMS** hails from Quebec, Canada, where she began performing Shakespeare as a teenager. After graduating from York University in Toronto with a B.F.A. degree, McAdams made her mark with the kiddie set on the TV series *The Famous Jett Jackson*. Movie audiences watched her go bad in *Mean Girls* and then soft and sweet as a girl choosing between two suitors in *The Notebook*. She has also starred in *The Family Stone*, and *Red Eye*, and caught Owen Wilson's glances in *Wedding Crashers*.

PAUL McGUIGAN

What in the world is better than *Chitty Chitty Bang Bang*? I'll never forget seeing it for the first time when I was a boy growing up in Scotland. Around Christmastime in our town, they would always show the same four movies—*The Sound of Music*, *Oliver!*, which I also adore, *The Great Escape*, and my favorite, *Chitty Chitty Bang Bang*. I'm not kidding when I say that I saw the same four movies every Christmas from the time I was a wee boy until I was eighteen! This was the big event.

I do remember the first time I went to the movie-house with my friends, and this car came out of nowhere. Suddenly, it was flying! Magic! My mother picked us up that day and all I could think was, *Our car doesn't do shit! It's not Chitty Chitty Bang Bang!*

I love the movie because it's really done through the eyes of a child. The filmmakers understood what it was like to be young. It's even a little bit scary. Remember the Child Catcher? This person lures children with lollipops away to a dungeon. It was actually frightening in a very fun way. But then you got back to the car, which was just the coolest thing ever.

Years later, when I became a director, I came to America to have a meeting with a Hollywood movie-studio executive. This man said to me, "Paul, is there any project you want to do? Tell us." I said, "Oh, I'd love to do a remake of *Chitty Chitty Bang Bang*." The studio exec got all excited. So, just to pull his leg, I continued on and said, "I want to call it *Chitty Chitty Bang Bang Boom!*" I just made that up off the top of my head. The younger executive in the room said to me,

"Dude, that's a great idea." Meanwhile, I was thinking, *Shut up! It's the dumbest idea ever. I'm pulling your leg.*

Oh, one more thing. I have two children now, and I love to watch this movie with them. I told them how, as a boy, Daddy had the Chitty Chitty Bang Bang toy, which was a car that had wings coming out of it. I thought this was just fantastic when I was little. My kids looked at me like I'm crazy. "What does it do, Dad?" they asked. With as much excitement as I could gather, I yell, "The wings! The wings come out of the car!" The kids just shrugged. I think there would have been more excitement if those wings came out of their iPod."

CHITTY CHITTY BANG BANG (1968). Children and adults alike wanted their own cars to fly through the air. Written by Roald Dahl and based on an Ian Fleming novel, this family classic features an eccentric professor who invents an extraordinary car that can fly. Dick Van Dyke stars as batty professor Caractacus Potts, who invents a car that draws the interest of a foreign government. Lionel Jeffries plays Grandpa Potts. Famous line from the Child Catcher: "There are children here somewhere. I can smell them!" The film's title song actually won an Oscar nomination.

Bellshill, Scotland, native **PAUL McGUIGAN** has directed several acclaimed indie films, including *Gangster No. 1*, *The Reckoning*, *Wicker Park*, and the critically acclaimed *Lucky Number Slevin*, which starred Morgan Freeman, Bruce Willis, and Josh Hartnett.

FERNANDO MEIRELLES

This is very hard to say. I'll say ten movies if you give me the chance. I've actually been asked this question before, and each time my answer is different depending on the day.

Today my answer is *Arabian Nights*. I love the structure of that film. It's a multiplot story, and you never know where the film will take you. I love the tone of the performances.

I don't like period films that feel like period films. I always see the actors performing. In that film you feel like you're in the period. You feel like you're in this place. It puts you there. I don't even exactly know why.

It's just a brilliant film. Someone is telling a story and inside the story is another story. Suddenly, you're inside the fifth story. The first character appears in the fifth story. It's really a brilliant structure. I also love the faces. We're not used to seeing Arabic types and people from North Africa in movies. They're really beautiful people, and it's a different type of beauty. In the end, everyone is so beautiful, and it's a gorgeous film.

ARABIAN NIGHTS (1942). The story of dancer Scheherazade and her efforts to fulfill what she believes to be her destiny—to become the wife of the kalif in Baghdad—stars Maria Montez and Sabu, with an assist from Jon Hall. The film scored Oscar nominations for its art direction, cinematography, music, and sound.

Brazil native **FERNANDO MEIRELLES** began working in independent TV. He made his mark directing *City of God* and the recent critically acclaimed *The Constant Gardener*.

NEIL MERON

Cabaret is it. I think it encapsulates everything I particularly love in musicals. It has a very compelling story with great characters. The brilliance of Bob Fosse has never been duplicated. There has never been anything better. There is something really powerful about *Cabaret*. It redefines movie musicals.

People think of musicals as happy confections that are sugarcoated. *Cabaret* blew the lid off that and gave you a stark feeling. It was unexpected to say the least.

Beyond that, all the writing and performances were superb. It has Bob and Liza. What more do you need? I love the scene where Liza and Michael York are under the train tracks, and she mentions that she likes to get everything out of her system. So, when the train goes overhead, she likes to scream. It's a fantastic scene.

CABARET (1972). In a near Oscar sweep, the musical about a bawdy cabaret singer named Sally Bowles took home gold for best director (Bob Fosse), actress (Liza Minnelli), supporting actor (Joel Grey), art direction, cinematography, editing, music, and sound. But it lost in the best picture and adapted screenplay categories. A decadent 1930s Berlin setting permeates the film dominated by Minnelli's voice and dance, with Grey supplying an extra dollop of decay as the omniscient master of ceremonies.

....

NEIL MERON has produced the Oscar-winning *Chicago*. He also produced *Gypsy, Cinderella, Annie, Life with Judy Garland: Me and My Shadows, The Music Man, The Reagans,* and the big-screen *Hairspray,* with John Travolta and Queen Latifah.

RYAN MERRIMAN

I love *Ferris Bueller's Day Off*. Oh my God, it's just a great movie with such a clever character. And there are the moments that you can't forget and many of them.

Who could forget the parade ride through Chicago, where Ferris grabs the microphone and sings "Twist and Shout"? But wait, before that there's Cameron's father's car. Cameron doesn't want to take the vintage car, but Ferris won't let him not take it. Later on they try to roll back the mileage, and I guarantee you every teen seeing that movie thought for a second, *That's a great idea. I wonder if that would really work in real life?*

Then you must remember how they try to put the car in reverse in the garage, it slips and then flies out the window. Horror and hilarious! I even like the mean sister, because in the end when the school principal breaks into her house and tries to get Ferris, she puts aside her jealous feelings and supports her brother. . . . I think the best part of Ferris is that you don't want it to be a movie. You want to be involved in their lives and be there with them.

FERRIS BUELLER'S DAY OFF (1986). Any trouble a kid can get into, Ferris Bueller gets into while taking a day off from high school. Matthew Broderick plays the student writer–director John Hughes immortalized, a kid who outsmarts his frustrated principal (Jeffrey Jones) and rules the day.

....

RYAN MERRIMAN is a former child actor from Oklahoma. He got his break on TV in the series *The Mommies*. His big-screen splash was playing Michelle Pfeiffer's grown-up, missing son in *The Deep End of the Ocean*. Merriman has also starred in *Just Looking, Halloween: Resurrection, The Ring Two, Final Destination 3,* and *Home of the Giants*.

MICHELLE MONAGHAN

I love *Steel Magnolias* because I love all those actresses. Come on! You have Sally Field, Shirley MacLaine, Olympia Dukakis, Dolly Parton, and Daryl Hannah. How could you lose?

I love to cry at movies. A good cry is a wonderful thing. So, my favorite scene in the movie is when Julia Roberts has died. Olympia and Shirley, as this character named Weezer, are at the funeral with Daryl, Sally, and Dolly. Sally says, "I'm so mad that my daughter died that I could hit somebody!" They say, "Well, hit Weezer!" It's funny and tragic at the same time.

I love that film so much because of all the great women. It was also one of the first films I saw when I was a kid. We didn't have cable and seldom went to the movies. But finally I saw this one great film and it has remained my favorite for years.

Those women made me laugh. They made me cry. They were mesmerizing. I think I love Dolly best of all. Just because she's Dolly. And just because I want to be her friend because she seems so sweet. But I'd stay away from Weezer!

STEEL MAGNOLIAS (1989). Robert Harling's play had room for a whole load of female performers sitting around Truvy's Beauty Parlor in Louisiana talking about their lives. Julia Roberts won a best supporting actress nomination in a cast that includes Dolly Parton as the salon owner, Sally Field, Shirley MacLaine, Daryl Hannah, Olympia Dukakis, Sam Shepard, and Tom Skerritt—all under Herb Ross's direction.

....

MICHELLE MONAGHAN is a dark-haired beauty who grew up near Cedar Rapids, Iowa, and studied journalism at Chicago's Columbia College. She got her start on TV in the series *Young Americans* and then arrived on the big screen with roles in *Perfume*, *Unfaithful*, *It Runs in the Family*, *The Bourne Supremacy*, *Kiss Kiss Bang Bang*, *Mr. & Mrs. Smith* (don't ask her about Brad and Angelina!), and *North Country*. She also starred opposite Tom Cruise in *Mission: Impossible III*.

MO'NIQUE

Oh my God, it's *Claudine*! It is just so real. It is honest-to-God real and fun at the same time. More than anything, Claudine is my story. It's the story of so many women I know, who like me come from Baltimore or any other city in America.

It's about a single mom who is struggling to raise her kids on welfare. That's the story of America. But because it stars Diahann Carroll, it has so much heart. Watching that movie is like wrapping myself up in a warm blanket.

I saw it as a kid. I saw it as a teenager, and I watch it now. I even have it on DVD. I love a story about a woman who triumphs over everything!

CLAUDINE (1974). Diahann Carroll won an Academy Award nomination for her role as the Harlem mother of six who's on welfare when she falls for a garbage man (James Earl Jones).

Baltimore native **MO'NIQUE** began her career doing stand-up comedy. She had roles on TV's *Moesha*, *The Hughleys*, and *The Parkers*. She has starred in such films as *Baby Boy*, *Two Can Play That Game*, *Soul Plane*, *Shadowboxer*, *Domino*, and *Phat Girlz*.

JULIANNE MOORE

This is the easiest question in the world. Clearly for me it's *Rosemary's Baby*. It's the best movie ever made about paranoia, and there's nothing I love better than a scary movie.

My favorite part is the end where poor Mia Farrow looks into that dark, forbidding cradle and says, "What have you done to his eyes?" then someone says to her—I think it's Ruth Gordon—but anyway, it's one of the devil people who say, "He has his father's eyes." The best part of all, unlike today's movies, you never see the baby. You never see those eyes. You don't even see the kid. I think today directors would have to create the perfect devil baby when in reality what you create in your mind, as an individual moviegoer, is the scariest thing of all. All you had in *Rosemary's Baby* was the mood, the faces of the adults, and that music that still scares the heck out of me.

And Mia. She's so young and vulnerable. Has anyone ever done young and vulnerable better? John Cassavetes. Amazing and wonderful.

I'll never forget that I saw this for the first time as a teenager. I didn't even get to see it in the theaters, but on TV, which was scary enough. I remember sitting there thinking, *This would even be one hundred times scarier in the theaters. Could I even take it?*

ROSEMARY'S BABY (1968). An unknown actor (John Cassavetes) trades his firstborn with Satan in return for a promising career without bothering to tell his wife (Mia Farrow). Roman Polanski directs the urban horror movie for which Ruth Gordon received a best supporting actress Oscar and Polanski's adapted screenplay took a nomination. During the course of the filming, Farrow chopped off most of her hair following an argument with husband Frank Sinatra. Polanski wrote it into the script.

·······································

Redheaded talent **JULIANNE MOORE** began her career on the TV soaps *The Edge of Night* and *As the World Turns*. Her early turns on the big screen include *Tales from the Darkside: The Movie, The Hand That Rocks the Cradle, Body of Evidence, Benny & Joon, The Fugitive, Short Cuts, Vanya on 42nd Street, Safe, Nine Months,* and *The Lost World: Jurassic Park.* She received an Oscar nomination for playing porn star Amber Waves in *Boogie Nights.* She has also starred in *The Big Lebowski,* a remake of *Psycho, A Map of the World,* and *The End of the Affair.* She replaced Jodie Foster as Clarice Starling in *Hannibal.* Her recent roles include *The Hours,* garnering her another Oscar nomination, *The Prize Winner of Defiance, Ohio; Trust the Man;* and *Children of Men.*

VIGGO MORTENSEN

There is a movie called *La Passion de Jeanne d'Arc*. I love it for many reasons, but start with the fact that the woman who plays Joan does it in such a raw way. It's beautifully acted with all of the dialogue in subtitles. Her performance is extraordinary and would stand up to any good acting today.

I also love that the director prepared for years to make the ultimate movie about Joan of Arc. He worked from all the transcripts of her trial, so those are the real words that we read in those subtitles. That's very beautiful and authentic to me, plus it really makes you sympathetic towards her.

His shooting technique was also interesting in that a lot of the film is shot in close-ups. The movie was made in 1928, and I can only imagine that at the time shooting this way must have seemed very disjointed. Now it's an accepted way to shoot. The entire movie was done in this grayish black and white, which covers Joan's face at times and just adds to the drama.

It's amazing to me when a movie holds up for that many years. You can still get the film on Criterion Home Video. They've even restored it to make it all that much more lovely. And let me say again that the actress who plays Joan—I can only remember that her first name is Maria [Maria Falconetti]—but she was extraordinary. She only did one movie. Some say she lost it doing this movie, and I can believe it.

It's all in the close-ups. She's really emotionally believable against the most heart-wrenching score. Her work holds up because she was gutsy and available. The perfect screen heroine of all time.

....

LA PASSION DE JEANNE D'ARC (1928). Maria Falconetti gives a breathtaking performance as Jeanne d'Arc, the famous martyr, in this black-and-white French version of the historical tale. Her anguished facial expressions are often done in close-up, where Falconetti conveys her pain with a simple leaning of her head or blink of her eyes. The silent French film follows the story of Joan as she is imprisoned, denied Communion, and eventually burned at the stake in the courtyard of Rouen Castle. Director Carl Theodor Dreyer's original vision of the film was a stark tale with no music, but the DVD version today features a score.

....

Great Dane **VIGGO MORTENSEN** grew up in New York with his Danish father and American mother. After graduating college he moved to Denmark, where he worked as a dockworker and sold flowers while writing and painting. In 1982 he returned to New York and worked on stage. His film career began with a role in *Witness* followed by *The Indian Runner, Carlito's Way, Crimson Tide, G.I. Jane, A Walk on the Moon, 28 Days, Hildalgo,* and *A History of Violence.* He's known internationally to a rabid Middle Earth fan base after playing King Aragorn in the Oscar-winning *The Lord of the Rings* trilogy. Mortensen is also an accomplished painter.

EMILY MORTIMER

I love *Saturday Night Fever*. Anyone who is making a big movie now should make one like this one because it's such a crowd pleaser. I love that this is a dance movie that's also about the acting and the writing. It's also a really raw movie and totally enjoyable.

I love the scene where John Travolta is getting ready for his night at the disco, but he has to eat dinner with his family. His father smacks him up in the head and he cries, "My hair! He touched my hair!" That's so funny. I also love a brilliant scene in the coffee shop with Karen Gorney as Stephanie. They're discussing the classics, and she seems all grand to him. She also thinks he's uncouth, which is hilarious, because she gets all the details wrong when she talks about *Romeo and Juliet*. It's a romantic, sad, and funny scene all rolled in one. The writing is so good.

If they made this movie today, it would be so commercial and saccharine.

SATURDAY NIGHT FEVER (1977). John Travolta donned a three-piece white suit and danced his way into movie history with his definitive screen portrait of Brooklyn mook Tony Manero. He won a best actor Oscar nomination for the role in John Badham's Bee Gees–fueled work about life in disco clubs. The film was based on Nik Cohn's magazine piece "Tribal Rites of the New Saturday Night."

British rose **EMILY MORTIMER** attended the prestigious St. Paul's Girls School in London with Oscar-winning actor Rachel Weisz. She made her small-screen debut on the mini-series *The Glass Virgin*. Her movie credits include *Elizabeth, Notting Hill, Scream 3, Love's Labour's Lost, The Kid, Lovely & Amazing, Bright Young Things, Dear Frankie, Match Point*, and *The Pink Panther*. She's married to actor Alessandro Nivola.

BILL PAXTON

One of my all-time favorites is *Splendor in the Grass*. It's a great unrequited love story written by the great playwright William Inge and directed by one of the masters, Elia Kazan.

It had Natalie Wood, who I was just crazy about, and a young Warren Beatty. Plus, it's a beautiful, tragic, sad story. The end is killer. She goes to visit him and his new wife looks just like her. The kid is on the floor playing with the chicken, and you're thinking, *Oh God, why isn't it their kid. Why is he playing with that chicken?* She says, "Are you happy, Bud?" He says, "I don't really think about that, Deenie."

Those are the kind of parts I want to do.

Another seminal film for me is *Harold and Maude*. I saw it when I first came to Hollywood from Fort Worth and I still can't get it out of my mind.

SPLENDOR IN THE GRASS (1961). Natalie Wood and Warren Beatty, in his screen debut, eventually became real-life lovers. But in playwright William Inge's Oscar-winning original screenplay, they played a tragic pair of teenagers whose lives were shattered by the sexual constraints of their time—the late 1920s and early 1930s in rural Kansas. In her Oscar-nominated role, Wood played a high school girl in love with a rich sports hero classmate. Warned by her puritanical mother not to "go all the way" with the boy, she makes a choice that drives her to the edge of madness and changes her life forever. Elia Kazan directed the bittersweet love story that was Inge's first written directly for the screen.

HAROLD AND MAUDE (1971). Hal Ashby's offbeat love story between a seventy-nine-year-old (Ruth Gordon) who loves life and a morbid twenty-year-old (Bud Cort) who's obsessed with death is considered a classic of the '70s. Listed on the National Film Registry, it stresses the value of life as seen through the eyes of a woman who is at the end of hers.

....

BILL PAXTON is an Everyman character actor who will forever be remembered for freaking out when told to put down his weapons in *Aliens.* "What are we supposed to use against them? Harsh language?" said his Private Hudson in a trembling voice. A Fort Worth, Texas, native who ditched the family lumber business to become a set decorator for Roger Corman, Paxton made his film debut in *Crazy Mama,* directed by Jonathan Demme. He has done roles in *The Terminator, Near Dark, Weird Science, One False Move, Tombstone, Apollo 13, True Lies, A Simple Plan, Twister,* and *Titanic.* Paxton currently stars on the hit HBO series *Big Love,* about a man trying to figure out how to keep his sanity when he has three demanding wives and a bevy of children.

DENNIS QUAID

I love *Lawrence of Arabia*. It's the most well-crafted epic ever made. David Lean takes you into the desert and makes you feel the heat and the sand. He makes you realize that movies can be larger than life. I can't stop watching this film. If I catch it on cable at three in the morning, I'm up for the rest of the night.

LAWRENCE OF ARABIA (1962). Playing the enigmatic T. E. Lawrence made Peter O'Toole an international star in David Lean's handsome, Oscar-winning epic depiction of Lawrence's desert adventures with an Arab leader. The film took home Oscars for best film, director (Lean), music (Maurice Jarre), art direction, cinematography, sound, and editing, but lost in the categories of best actor (O'Toole), supporting actor (Omar Sharif), and adapted screenplay.

DENNIS QUAID is a Houston, Texas, native who began his career starring in the 1979 youth classic *Breaking Away*. He received raves in his early career playing astronaut Gordon Cooper in *The Right Stuff*. He has also starred in *The Big Easy, Innerspace, Suspect, D.O.A., Everybody's All-American, Great Balls of Fire!, Postcards from the Edge, Wyatt Earp, The Parent Trap, Any Given Sunday, The Rookie, Far from Heaven, The Alamo, The Day After Tomorrow,* and *In Good Company*. He directed *Everything That Rises*. He played The King of Western Swing, musician Spade Cooley, in *Shame on You*, which he also directed.

DANIEL RADCLIFFE

Of course, my favorite movie is *12 Angry Men*. All that angst! All that drama! I just love it! It deals with everything that's important. You have to determine the truth, which is what we all do on a daily basis in life. I also love Henry Fonda's performance. He makes me want to be a better actor and do my own version of *12 Angry Men* someday.

12 ANGRY MEN (1957). The power of one man to sway a jury bent on convicting a defendant based on their preconceptions is what makes Sidney Lumet's Oscar-nominated film a perpetual favorite. Henry Fonda heads the impressive cast that includes Lee J. Cobb, E. G. Marshall, Jack Klugman, Ed Begley, and Jack Warden in bringing the Reginald Rose screenplay to life. Lumet and Rose also were nominated for Academy Awards.

DANIEL RADCLIFFE is Harry Potter in one of the most popular film franchises of all time. The teen hails from London and beat out thousands of young actors to play the boy wizard. Of course, he hopes to direct someday.

HAROLD RAMIS

I could be on the same bandwagon as the other guys and say *Bridge on the River Kwai*. Did they say that movie? I think David Lean made some extraordinary movies.

But I love Scorsese, and my favorite film was *Goodfellas*. I read the book when it was called *Wise Guys*. He couldn't use that title because they made a comedy called *Wise Guys*. Just a fun fact.

Goodfellas is like counterprogramming to *The Godfather*. That's the mythic, poetic version of organized crime. But *Goodfellas* is the reality of organized crime. It was about stealing cigarettes. It was about getting shot. These guys were pretty violent, and it was not glamorous at all. *The Godfather* was like an opera compared to that.

By the way, Lorraine Bracco will never be better. There was a stridency to the character that really worked. There was desperation. I love Ray Liotta in the movie—and De Niro is brilliant. I've had this conversation with De Niro. We've said, "People aren't perfect and aren't lovable all the time. They don't always do the right thing. That's what makes them human."

I know Scorsese's view of New York is much more realistic. You feel like you were really there. He was really able to depict that life. I also love *Taxi Driver*. Scorsese created that reality by using actors that made it hyperreal.

These are great movies.

GOODFELLAS (1990). Nobody does Mob violence the way director Martin Scorsese does, and this film version of small-time mobster

Henry Hill's true story is a prime example. With Oscar nominations for best picture, director, supporting actress (Lorraine Bracco), editing, and screenplay, it scored only for Joe Pesci, named best supporting actor for his ultraviolent portrait of the vicious Tommy DeVito. Ray Liotta starred as Hill, who eventually ratted out his friends, while Robert De Niro co-starred as a gangster on his way up, no matter what it takes.

TAXI DRIVER (1976). Shocking for its time, Martin Scorsese's drama about a crazed New York cabbie (Robert De Niro) infatuated with a political worker (Cybill Shepherd) and a child prostitute (Jodie Foster) won no Oscars despite nominations for best picture, lead actor (De Niro), supporting actress (Foster), and music (Bernard Herrmann).

Chicago native and former ghostbuster **HAROLD RAMIS** cut his teeth on *Second City TV*. As an actor, he starred in *Stripes, Ghostbusters, Baby Boom, Stealing Home, Ghostbusters II, Groundhog Day, Love Affair, As Good As It Gets, High Fidelity*, and *Orange County*. He wrote *Animal House, Meatballs, Caddyshack, Back to School*, and *Analyze That*. Ramis also directed *Caddyshack, Vacation, Groundhog Day, Stuart Saves His Family, Multiplicity, Analyze This, Bedazzled, Analyze That*, and *The Ice Harvest*.

BRETT RATNER

My favorite film is *Being There* by Hal Ashby. I loved it because it was a comedy that was shot like a drama. It was also such a moving film that made you laugh and made you cry. You go through every emotion and fall in love with the characters.

Chauncey Gardiner. Who is better?

I've watched it a million times. My favorite part is when he walks on water at the end. In what's a fun film, you go to this place that's so deep.

What I got out of it was the idea that if you don't know you can't do something, you can do it. The fact that he didn't know he could walk on water meant he could do it. It was just such a beautiful and touching ending to me.

I heard a great story about this movie concerning director Robert Downey Sr. Hal called him up and said, "Robert you did a film called *Greaser's Palace* where you have a scene where someone walks on water. Do you mind if I steal it from you?" Robert replied, "You're not stealing it from me. You're stealing it from the Bible."

BEING THERE (1979). Critics began to take comedian Peter Sellers seriously once he embodied Chance, the simple gardener whose every word is treated like something profound once he leaves his master's estate. Sellers was nominated for an Oscar, but it was supporting actor Melvyn Douglas who won for his work in the film.

....

Miami native **BRETT RATNER** directs the successful *Rush Hour* fran-
chise with Jackie Chan and Chris Tucker. After getting his start at NYU
Film School and directing music videos for Madonna and Mariah
Carey, he stepped behind the camera to helm films such as *The Family
Man, Red Dragon, After the Sunset,* and X-Men: *The Last Stand*.

JONATHAN RHYS MEYERS

There's a film I love called *The Bicycle Thief*. Woody Allen, who I just worked with, loves it, too. It's just a great, great movie. I just like the whole concept of it and loved the way it was shot. I couldn't take my eyes off the screen.

I saw it at a big cinema in Los Angeles. *The Bicycle Thief* was playing before this other movie. I was just enraptured. This was ten years ago. Every so often I still get images from it. You see those images in the careers of Woody and Martin Scorsese. Many of those guys learned from that movie.

I suppose it's not even the starkness of that movie that gets me. It's the simplicity. It's a very simple story told in a basic way. At the end of the day that's what every director wants to do: tell a simple story as simply as possible. If you try to layer something with unnecessary complexities, you're just clogging your head. The simpler things like *The Bicycle Thief* are the most dumbfounding, the most natural, and the most beautiful.

I also like *Good Will Hunting*. It's a simple story. There is nothing hugely complex about *Good Will Hunting*. It doesn't have the weight of a Pulitzer Prize–winning novel. It's also two talented actors—Ben Affleck and Matt Damon—at the right time with the right script. Robin Williams also gave an outstanding performance as the doctor. By the time the film ended, you knew what would happen. You knew what would happen the whole time. But I didn't care.

....

THE BICYCLE THIEF (1948). When film professors discuss classic Italian cinema, Vittorio De Sica's Oscar-winning drama is always mentioned. Awarded Oscars for best foreign-language film and its screenplay, it traces the desperation of a man whose bike is stolen just before he is to start his first job in two years.

GOOD WILL HUNTING (1997). The breakthrough film for Matt Damon and Ben Affleck, who shared a best screenplay Oscar, this is the story of a math genius working as a janitor (Damon) who works with a shrink (Robin Williams) to come to terms with his brilliance. He must also figure out what to do with his blue-collar friends (including Affleck) who have their own issues and a beautiful medical student (Minnie Driver).

....

JONATHAN RHYS MEYERS was reared in County Cork, Ireland. The sexy young star played the King of Rock 'n' Roll in the TV movie *Elvis* and had roles in the movies *Vanity Fair, I'll Sleep When I'm Dead, Bend It Like Beckham, Titus, Velvet Goldmine,* and *Michael Collins.* He recently starred for director Woody Allen in *Match Point* and opposite Tom Cruise in *Mission: Impossible III.*

ANNASOPHIA ROBB

I really love the first *Harry Potter* and the *Lord of the Rings* movies. I read all the books in both of those series. I just love to read fantasy, and both of the movies were really good. The movies took you to these other worlds that were totally different. That's what I want in a movie. Just take me away.

I love the first *Harry Potter* because you meet Harry and you see that he has a real world with his horrible aunt and uncle, but he also has his secret world of magic. I love all the characters, especially Ron and Hermoine, his best friends.

Now, I love the *Lord of the Rings* people, too. I love, love, love Orlando Bloom. He's a little cutie. I think I would follow him into Middle Earth, but please don't tell my mom. I'd only do this, Mom, if I trained to defend myself so I wouldn't get hurt. Okay? Of course, I could stay back with Liv Tyler, who played the beautiful Elf princess Arwen. That was such a good love story, between the Elf princess and the future king, played by Viggo Mortensen. Notice that Orlando didn't have a girlfriend in Middle Earth. I'm just mentioning it. I did like how Liv and Viggo had a little kiss. That was perfect. I don't like big gross love scenes.

Oh, the Gollum was kinda cool, too. He's a little monster, but has something deep in his heart that's sweet. But he still has that creepy, kill-y side. I guess I wouldn't want to run into him. My mom would be pretty worried.

HARRY POTTER AND THE SORCERER'S STONE (2001). The introduction of the boy wizard Harry, who must battle the forces of evil that resulted in his parents' deaths, is made in this Chris Columbus film detailing the boy's days at Hogwarts School of Witchcraft and Wizardry. A whole slew of Potter characters join the fray as Harry enters his first Quidditch match. The film picked up Oscar nominations for its art direction, costumes, and music.

THE LORD OF THE RINGS: THE FELLOWSHIP OF THE RING (2001). The first of Peter Jackson's J. R. R. Tolkien trilogy adaptations introduces Hobbits, Frodo, and the forces they will have to battle in order to find an ancient ring that will determine the fate of many. Although the film received Oscars for cinematography, visual effects, makeup, and music, it lost in the categories of supporting actor (Ian McKellen), art direction, costuming, director, editing, original song, sound, screenplay, original song, and best picture.

....

ANNASOPHIA ROBB grew up in Denver, Colorado. At age ten, she was seen by millions in the lead role of Opal with Jeff Daniels in *Because of Winn-Dixie*. She has guest starred on *Drake & Josh* and played the lead in *Samantha: An American Girl Story*, with Mia Farrow. On the big screen, Anna can be seen in *Charlie and the Chocolate Factory* and *Doubting Thomas*.

BRIAN ROBBINS

When I was a little boy, my dad, Floyd Robbins, was in a movie called *The Hot Rock* with Robert Redford. My dad brought me to the set, and I got to sit in Robert Redford's lap. I was five or six. Let's just say that years later when I went to see *Butch Cassidy and the Sundance Kid*, I was already a huge Redford fan. I love *Butch Cassidy*. I love those guys and the whole fantasy of it. There were no rules in their world. Remember when they have a knife fight. It's "One, two, three . . . fight." My favorite scene is when they rob the train and then these guys come after them. Next comes the big chase and they have to jump. You know the fall will probably kill them.

It's just a great movie with that perfect bittersweet ending. You know they're going to die, but you didn't see it. If this movie were made today, you would have seen them blown to pieces. And that's wrong. I think it's better when you just can't fill in all the blanks.

But wait, I have to say one more film, which is *Trading Places*, which I'll team with *48 Hours*. I guess that's two more favorite films, but I can't take either of them out. These were both brilliant comedic movies starring the amazing Eddie Murphy at the beginning of his brilliant career. The premise of *Trading Places* was genius—just a simple role reversal, but perfect. Dan Aykroyd is frickin' amazing and can I say it one more time? Eddie was amazing. Those are the comedies that made me want to make comedies one day.

BUTCH CASSIDY AND THE SUNDANCE KID (1969). George Roy Hill's classic four-time Oscar-winning Western stars Robert Redford and Paul Newman as two bank and train robbers who must flee to Bolivia when a posse of lawmen gets too close for comfort. Famous quote from the Sundance Kid: "What I'm saying is, if you want to go, I won't stop you. But the minute you start to whine or make a nuisance, I don't care where we are, I'm dumping you flat."

TRADING PLACES (1983). Here's a young Eddie Murphy as Billy Ray Valentine, a street con artist who changes stations in life with two calculating millionaires, played by Ralph Bellamy and Don Ameche. It also marks one of Jamie Lee Curtis's early film roles as a hooker with a heart of gold. Is there any other kind?

48 HRS. (1982). Eddie Murphy is a con named Reggie who is sprung from jail for two days to team up with a hotheaded, alcoholic San Francisco cop named Jack Cates, played by Nick Nolte. Together they must track down a killer while the clock is ticking.

·····································

Brooklyn native **BRIAN ROBBINS** began his career as a teen heart-throb on the popular series *Head of the Class* and then hosted the kiddie version of *Pictionary*. He stopped emoting to step behind the camera as the director of several $100-million-plus hits, including *The Shaggy Dog*, *Varsity Blues*, and *Hard Ball*.

ROBERT RODRIGUEZ

I put on a lot of movies when I'm editing, I don't watch them completely, but I find inspiration in them. One of my favorite movies of all time is *Glengarry Glen Ross*. *Heat* is another one.

I love the moment in *Heat* when Pacino and De Niro get together in that restaurant. They shot that one with two cameras. The tension is there. The dialogue is great. You have two great actors bouncing it up and back with each other. You can watch that one scene a million times.

I love *Glengarry Glen Ross* because my dad is a salesman and the movie reminds me of that world. I looked at that movie to find the character of Frank in *Sin City*. I love the lines: "I had to sell him." And I love Jack Lemmon. I can't take my eyes off him.

GLENGARRY GLEN ROSS (1992). James Foley directed this acclaimed drama written by David Mamet about life in a real estate office and a sales contest that separates the losers from the closers. It's easy to be sold on a cast that includes Jack Lemmon, Al Pacino, Ed Harris, Alan Arkin, Kevin Spacey, Alec Baldwin, and Jonathan Pryce.

HEAT (1995). Al Pacino and Robert De Niro clashed in a delicious way in the Michael Mann–directed tale of a cop, Lt. Vincent Hanna (Pacino), and a robber, Neil McCauley (Robert De Niro), who have a head-on collision. De Niro's team included baddies played by Val Kilmer, Jon Voight, and Tom Sizemore, with Ashley Judd onboard as Kilmer's crafty wife who gives him a signal to drive away from his impending arrest. Pacino is married to Diane Venora and plays a step-dad to her messed-up daughter (Natalie Portman). The classic scene is in a coffee shop where De Niro and Pacino meet. Pacino to De Niro: "Brother, you are going down."

....

Texan **ROBERT RODRIGUEZ** delivers great films on low, low budgets. He grew up in San Antonio, where he began drawing cartoons and making movies as a child. In 1992 he became a legend in Hollywood when he directed the small film *El Mariachi*, made on a shoestring budget, and edited the film at a public-access station in Austin. He even wrote a book about it called *Rebel Without a Crew*. He has also written, directed, and produced *Desperado*, *From Dusk Till Dawn*, *The Faculty*, *Spy Kids*, *Once Upon a Time in Mexico*, and *Sin City*. His regular acting troupe includes Antonio Banderas, Salma Hayek, Cheech Marin, Danny Trejo, and Robert Patrick. His cast insists he makes great Mexican food on the set.

RAY ROMANO

I'm just a huge fan of the original *Rocky*. I'll never forget that I was eighteen when that movie came out. I remember that I was coaching a Little League team of twelve-year-olds at the time to make some extra money. But I really got into the season, and we made it down to the wire. It was between us and one other team.

So, I took all the twelve-year-olds on my team to see *Rocky* the night before our big championship game. They walked out of there pumped up! Eye of the tiger! Well, maybe that was *Rocky* 2 or 3. But they were saying, "Yo, Ray, we can do it!"

We lost by eight points. But we were still inspired to do great things in life. We saw *Rocky*.

ROCKY (1976). An unknown actor with an offbeat appeal, Sylvester Stallone turned into an overnight success playing the title role of a small-time Philadelphia boxer named Rocky Balboa who just wanted to go the distance. Stallone wrote it sitting on a milk crate in his run-down New York apartment. When a studio became interested in Stallone's underdog-themed script, he refused to sell it unless he could star in it. The rest is box-office history, and a string of *Rocky* movies starred the sluggish-voiced Stallone, who never really escaped the character. The film, directed by John G. Avildsen, won Oscars for best picture, best director, and best editing. But Stallone failed to win as best actor or original screenwriter. Also on the losing end were Talia Shire as best actress, Burt Young and Burgess Meredith in the supporting actor category, plus the film's music and sound. Stallone became the third person nominated in both acting and writing categories in the same year, following in the footsteps of Charlie Chaplin for *The Great Dictator* and Orson Welles for *Citizen Kane*.

....

RAY ROMANO is a man who can't resist a punch line. The New York native played Ray Barone on the CBS hit *Everybody Loves Raymond* for nine seasons. He also executive-produced the series, which earned him a slew of Emmys and worldwide fame. He began his career in various stand-up clubs, figuring if he could make his friends laugh, then maybe strangers would pay him for the same thing. While hitting open-mike clubs around New York, he continued to work as a futon mattress deliveryman and bank teller by day. Eventually he quit his day job. David Letterman became a fan of his act and offered Romano a development deal through his production company, Worldwide Pants. The rest is history, including movie roles (*Eulogy, Welcome to Mooseport*), books, and a comedy album, *Live at Carnegie Hall*. He also voiced the woolly mammoth Manny in the hit films *Ice Age* and *Ice Age 2: The Meltdown*.

GENA ROWLANDS

Oh, there are so many. . . . So many. How can I possibly choose? I'm a huge fan of *Dark Victory*. I don't think you're allowed to forget Bette Davis walking up those stairs. How could you possible forget her? She burned that scene into your mind, which is the mark of great acting.

DARK VICTORY (1939). No one plays tragedy the way Bette Davis did, and here she pulls out all the stops as a socialite and horsewoman diagnosed with a deadly brain tumor. Davis received an Oscar nomination for her role as a woman trying to live life to the fullest while she can. Her character takes that determination too far once she realizes she has no chance of survival despite the love of her surgeon (George Brent). With only six months to live, and in one of cinema's most dramatic endings, she begins to lose her sight as death beckons. The film was also nominated for best picture and best music.

GENA ROWLANDS is a screen legend who was married to a screen legend—John Cassavetes. Together they made ten movies, including *A Child Is Waiting*, *Faces*, *Gloria*, *Opening Night*, *A Woman Under the Influence*, *Two-Minute Warning*, and *Tempest*. She also starred in *Lonely Are the Brave*, *Tony Rome*, *The Brink's Job*, *Once Around*, and *The Notebook*, directed by her son, Nick Cassavetes.

KURT RUSSELL

Casablanca is my favorite film. It's the most emotionally satisfying film ever made and has the best dialogue in any movie ever. It's also the greatest romantic film. I love it because it's about something, too. In my mind, the message is about people facing their moment of truth. We've all been there or will be there in our real lives.

By the way, the people starring in the best movie of all time are as good as it gets. The words they said have never been rivaled by any other film. You just can't improve on them.

Anytime I see *Casablanca* on TV, I'm stuck. I'm going to watch the entire thing.

CASABLANCA (1942). Winner of the Oscars for best picture, best director (Michael Curtiz), and best screenplay, this bittersweet love story is set against the backdrop of World War II in Africa. Humphrey Bogart immortalized the character of café owner Rick Blaine, a guy who fell in love with a woman (Ingrid Bergman) who deserted him in Paris. The film's famed theme is "As Time Goes By," and, yes, Bogart tells the piano player to "play it again."

KURT RUSSELL got his start at age ten doing a small role in the Elvis film *It Happened at the World's Fair*. Walt Disney signed him to a ten-year contract. After playing minor league baseball, he went back to the big screen with roles in *The Thing, Silkwood, Escape from New York, Swing Shift, The Mean Season, Overboard, Backdraft, Tombstone, Escape from L.A., Dark Blue,* and *Poseidon*.

ADAM SANDLER

Oh God, it's so easy. I love *The Wizard of Oz*. This is not exactly the kind of thing a man wants to admit, but my mother makes me watch it again and again. Okay, that's not exactly true. I want to watch it, too. Maybe I even make my mother watch it with me. Now the secret is out. But don't you think Dorothy is pretty cute and that Scarecrow had a heart from the beginning, if you ask me.

THE WIZARD OF OZ (1939). Though it didn't win the biggest award on Oscar night, it was nominated for best picture and managed to snag statuettes for its original score and original song, "Over the Rainbow." No one else in the beloved musical—not Judy Garland as Dorothy, the girl from Kansas; not Bert Lahr as the Cowardly Lion; not Ray Bolger as the Scarecrow; and not Jack Haley as the Tin Man—was nominated. The film airs regularly on television as new generations respond to the fantasy tale of a girl spun into the air along with her dog, Toto, and deposited in the Land of Oz. If she wants to get home, she has to "follow the yellow brick road" and go "off to see the Wizard."

ADAM SANDLER is a Brooklyn native who got his start as a Not Ready For Primetime Player on *Saturday Night Live*. He has starred in the movies *Coneheads*, *Airheads*, *Mixed Nuts*, *Billy Madison*, *Harry Gilmore*, *The Wedding Singer*, *The Waterboy*, *Big Daddy*, *Anger Management*, *50 First Dates*, and *The Longest Yard*. He took a dramatic turn in *Punch-Drunk Love* and *Spanglish*. Sandler also lent his voice, produced, and helped write the animated Hanukkah comedy *Eight Crazy Nights*.

PETER SARSGAARD

There is a documentary that came out that I really liked called *Wheel of Time*. Let me first say that as an actor, documentaries have a lot more impact often than other films. Werner Herzog came out with a few films recently, including *Grizzly Man*. He also did *The White Diamond*, which was pretty great, too.

But this one called *Wheel of Time* was about the Buddhists doing the Mandalas for days. When they're done, the Dalai Lama takes it from them; they put it in a vase and dump it into the river. They've spent a week making this fine drawing. It's very funny to see Werner, who is such a skeptic, talking to the Dalai Lama. It's amazing to see those personalities clashing.

I also love that this is a different movie about Buddhist monks. Usually they look like children in movies, but in this one they're someone you can relate to. Werner is looking for the parts in the monks that are like him. For example, when do they fight? But they do in the movie. They fight in this great way. You see them arguing about the whole duality thing. Do they need to argue about it again? It's the craziest thing you've ever seen, but it's so nice to see them argue. Good to know you guys don't just meditate.

WHEEL OF TIME (2003). Werner Herzog directed this documentary about Tibetan Buddhist rituals and an initiation taking place in India where the masses gather.

....

Illinois native **PETER SARSGAARD** recently starred in the back-to-back hits *Jarhead* and *Flight Plan*. He has also appeared in *Dead Man Walking*, *The Man in the Iron Mask*, *Desert Blue*, *Another Day in Paradise*, *Boys Don't Cry*, *The Cell*, *Housebound*, *Empire*, *The Salton Sea*, *K-19: The Widowmaker*, *Shattered Glass*, *Garden State*, *Kinsey*, and *The Skeleton Key*.

LIEV SCHREIBER

I have two favorite films. The first is *Time of the Gypsies*. It's a wonderful film by one of the greatest filmmakers of all time, Emir Kusturica. It's a wonderful story about a gypsy with strange powers who leads a life of crime. It's just one of those movies where you can't stop watching because it's so interesting.

I also love *Being There* by Hal Ashby. I think I've always been kind of drawn to the psychology of isolation and the idea of innocence. What is it about the character of Chance played by Peter Sellers? He just really gets me. I love his detachment and his ability to not only exist, but also thrive on his detachment. That's really, really appealing to me. I don't just love his character, but love the whole movie. It's beautiful at the end when he walks by the water, but then again, every scene is so wonderful. When the press visits and Chance mutters insane things about gardening and preserving plants . . . it's amazing. The movie is simple and very magical.

TIME OF THE GYPSIES (1988). Emir Kusturica directs Davor Dujmovic in the tale of a Romany gypsy with telekinetic powers who falls into a life of petty crime in Serbia.

BEING THERE (1979). Critics began to take comedian Peter Sellers seriously once he embodied Chance, the simple gardener whose every word is treated like something profound once he leaves his master's estate. Sellers was nominated for an Oscar, but it was supporting actor Melvyn Douglas who won for his work in the film.

....

Pronounced *Lee-ev*, six-foot-three consummate actor **LIEV SCHREIBER** grew up in New York, where he is the son of Tell Schreiber, a theater actor who also worked in film. His mother is a painter who worked as a cab driver in the Big Apple. Schreiber grew up at his local revival house because his mother didn't want him to see color films as a child and teenager. After studying at Yale School of Drama, he began his career on stage and later won a Tony Award for *Glengarry Glen Ross*. His movie career includes *Walking and Talking, The Daytrippers, Big Night, Scream, Scream 2, A Walk on the Moon, Jakob the Liar, The Sum of All Fears*, and *The Manchurian Candidate*. He recently directed *Everything Is Illuminated*.

JOEL SCHUMACHER

I'd have to choose *Great Expectations*. The David Lean version. Of course, I didn't know who David Lean was at the time I saw the movie—or who Charles Dickens was. I saw the movie when I was seven. I grew up behind the Sunnyside movie theater in Long Island City before television was invented. Even when television came out we were too poor. My father was dead and it was just my mother and I. And she was out at work all the time.

I was this kid like in *Cinema Paradiso* who had to be yanked out of the movie theater. I lived in the movie theater.

And when I was seven, I saw *Great Expectations*. The David Lean version. What I think happened in an armchair analysis of it, I had seen so many movies already in my life. But this one began with a little boy, Pip, in a graveyard. I think from that first image I saw me because my father was dead and I was a little boy without a father who had been to the cemetery.

That film is about a poor boy with great expectations. After that was when I decided I wanted to make movies. I knew someone was making these stories. I didn't know how. But I knew I wanted to tell these stories. Of course, that would have to be my favorite.

GREAT EXPECTATIONS (1946). David Lean brought the classic Dickens tale to the big screen, starring Anthony Wager as a young Pip and John Mills as the older Pip. The tale chronicles the adventures of an orphan and the strange types who enter his life, including a bitter woman named Miss Havisham (Martita Hunt), who helps raise him and her other charge, Estella (Valerie Hobson).

....

New York native **JOEL SCHUMACHER** began his career studying at Parsons School of Design in New York but quickly changed his focus to film directing. Known for making stars out of total unknowns, he launched the career of Demi Moore in *St. Elmo's Fire*, Julia Roberts in *Flatliners* and *Dying Young*, and Colin Farrell in *Tigerland*. He has also directed *Falling Down, The Client, Batman Forever, A Time to Kill*, and *Phone Booth*.

MARTIN SCORSESE

I love so many movies, but these are a few of my favorite. I love the original *Scarface* from 1932. It caused quite a stir with its extraordinary violence, which, let's face it, is something I know about from my own films. The thing about *Scarface* is not just the violence, but the way the bloodshed was directed by Howard Hawks. What I love is the idea that Paul Muni portrayed a fierce man named Tony Camonte, but you really like this guy. He's dangerous, but you actually love him. That's the same thing I tried to do with the main characters in *Goodfellas*.

I love the scene in *Scarface* where they're all sitting there in a coffee shop and suddenly all of these cars drive up. You just know there is going to be a few funerals as a result. These men are in long coats and they're carrying machine guns. They kneel down and they just spray the place with machine-gun bullets. What makes me laugh is that while people are dropping dead all around him, Muni is going, "What kind of guns do they have? Hey, look at those things. That's a lot of bullet power. It's so interesting, those guns. . . ." Next, he tells George Raft, who plays Guino, "Go get me one!" Suddenly, Muni shoots a few guys. Bullets are flying. It's actually very fun until director Howard Hawks brings you back to reality by showing two or three of the older men being hit by bullets and dropping dead. Meanwhile, the maniac gunmen are still thrilled. One screams, "Look at this! It's terrific."

I think the embracing of these guys and this world is very dangerous, but thrilling.

You must also let me say that William Wellman's *Public Enemy* is one of my favorites. There the characters aren't very likable. I take that back because anyone would like Jimmy Cagney as Tom Powers, but that's not the point. Oh my God, I can't even think of this film without seeing blood. It's brutal, tough, truthful, and honest. And there is no score. It's music coming off radio or record players, which is very real.

In fact, I showed the film to Leonardo DiCaprio, who invited a few of his friends to this screening room at my house. There was spontaneous applause at the end of the film. I said, "Oh, I wish William Wellman was here to see twenty-five-year-old kids shocked and stunned and applauding his great work seventy-five years later." I looked at Leo and said, "Someday, you need to top that and it's not in the bullet work. What makes this movie soar is the attitude."

·······································

SCARFACE (1932). Howard Hawks directed this violent gangster drama about a man trying to move up the ladder in the Mob. Watch the bodies pile up in this brutal classic. It stars Paul Muni as lisping trigger man Antonio "Tony" Camonte and George Raft as Guino Rinaldo. Boris Karloff also shows up as Gaffney. Best line from Inspector Ben Guarino: "I told you you'd show up this way. Get you in a jam without a gun and you squeal like a yellow rat."

THE PUBLIC ENEMY (1931). James Cagney and Jean Harlow star in the story of a small-time crook who goes big time during prohibition. It's the movie that contains Cagney's famous grapefruit-in-his-girlfriend's-face scene and is part of the National Film Registry. It won an Oscar nomination for its original screenplay.

·······································

More than anyone in the movie industry, filmmaking great **MARTIN SCORSESE** deserves an Oscar. The premiere director of his generation once thought about entering the priesthood. His life took a different turn when he graduated from NYU as a film major. He made his big-screen directorial debut with *Who's That Knocking at My Door*. Scorsese went on to direct some of the best gritty street classics in movie history, including *Mean Streets, Taxi Driver, Goodfellas*, and *Casino*, plus the musical *New York, New York* and the black comedy

The King of Comedy. His trademark style focuses on New York and the loners who navigate the pavements in the Big Apple. He has also directed *Alice Doesn't Live Here Anymore, After Hours, The Color of Money, The Last Temptation of Christ, Cape Fear, The Age of Innocence, Kundun, Bringing Out the Dead, Gangs of New York, The Aviator*, and *The Departed*. He received an American Film Institute Life Achievement Award in 1997. Look for his late parents, Charles and Catherine, in several of his movies. His mother played Joe Pesci's mama in *Goodfellas*, and she cooked the food for the scene.

JIM SHERIDAN

There is just one choice. *The Godfather*. It's just a magnificent movie, you know. It's a family saga, and I love a family saga. It's got everything—great acting, visually brilliant, wonderful cinematography. I also love Spielberg, and my favorite film of his is *E.T.* He's just such a brilliant creature to teach you about life and love. He wants what we all want . . . to go home. I also love that it's serious, but it's a popcorn movie as well. I tend not to like big intellectual movies. I'd rather have a subtle story with a warm story. And *E.T.* is just a great, warm story.

THE GODFATHER (1972). Francis Ford Coppola's Mafia saga begins when the aging Don Vito Corleone (Marlon Brando) of the Corleone Mob family transfers his control to his son Michael (Al Pacino), although the World War II vet just wants to lead a normal life. James Caan plays the doomed Sonny with John Cazale as Fredo. Diane Keaton is Michael's love interest Kay. Best line: "Leave the gun. Take the cannolis."

E.T. THE EXTRA-TERRESTRIAL (1982). Steven Spielberg created this masterpiece story of a small creature named E.T. who is the original illegal alien. He gets stranded in suburbia, and a bunch of Earth children help him "go home." Drew Barrymore is at her most adorable as E.T.'s little friend Gertie. Her brother Elliott played by Henry Thomas is heartbreaking when he must let his friend go forever.

·······································

Irish director **JIM SHERIDAN** runs his own production company, Hell's Kitchen. The acclaimed director has called the shots on such movies as the Oscar-nominated *My Left Foot*, which won the best actor Oscar for star Daniel Day-Lewis and best supporting actress for Brenda Fricker as his mother. He has also directed *The Field, In the Name of the Father, The Boxer, In America,* and *Get Rich or Die Trying.*

JOHN SINGLETON

The Seven Samurai is my favorite film. There's just so much action, humor, and drama with great, great characters. It shows you how films can be so universal. It's a Japanese film done in Japanese, but it plays so well everywhere in the world.

I love the part when one of the characters comes out of this place where they've taken the farmer's wife. She knows she's been shamed. The bandits kidnapped her, and they took all the women. They don't show what they do to the women. You can just guess. In the Japanese culture, that's shame.

After the shame, this woman sees her husband. He's sad and everything, and she runs back into the fire. He can't run back into the fire to save her. Their baby is there, too. One of the Samurai saves the baby, and then he breaks down and cries.

It's one of the most emotional scenes you've ever seen.

THE SEVEN SAMURAI (1954). Japanese filmmaker Akira Kurosawa's acclaimed masterwork, this is a much-imitated but rarely equaled drama about a village that hires samurai to help fend off marauding bandits. In return for food, the warriors teach the villagers how to fight back. Toshirô Mifune emerged from the film a major star while its costume and art direction received Oscar nominations. If the plot seems familiar, take a look at *The Magnificent Seven*. It's a Westernized version of the same movie.

••••••••••••••••••••••••••••••••

Writer-producer-director **JOHN SINGLETON** grew up in Los Angeles, where he got his break at the Filmic Writing Program at USC. He directed and wrote the breakthrough street film *Boyz n the Hood*. He also directed *Poetic Justice, Higher Learning, Rosewood, Shaft, Baby Boy, 2 Fast 2 Furious, Four Brothers*, and *Luke Cage*. He produced the hit films *Hustle & Flow* and *Black Snake Moan*.

IMELDA STAUNTON

Oh God, this is hard, but one of my favorite films that I saw when I was underage was *The Graduate*. It was such an important film, and I couldn't wait to see it. Mr. Hoffman was the pinup on my school locker door. You could say he made quite an impression on me. It was my first racy film, but I thought it was semi-innocent with some debauchery on the side.

I saw it for the first time at a local cinema in London. At the time, I wanted to be Mrs. Robinson. God, what a wonderful woman. What a beautiful, wonderful, wonderful woman.

THE GRADUATE (1967). With its Simon and Garfunkel song as famous as its plot, the Mike Nichols film about life after college graduation ranks as an American classic. Dustin Hoffman stars as Benjamin Braddock, a guy who falls for the daughter of his father's disapproving partner. On top of everything else, the partner's wife, Mrs. Robinson (Anne Bancroft), seduces the boy, who really wants her daughter (Katharine Ross). Nichols took home a directing Oscar, but the movie lost out on its lead actor (Hoffman), actress (Bancroft), supporting actress (Ross), cinematography, screenplay, and best picture nominations.

London native **IMELDA STAUNTON** has starred in such movies as *Sense and Sensibility*, *Shakespeare in Love*, *Chicken Run*, and *Crush*. She was nominated for an Oscar for her role in *Vera Drake*. Staunton has also starred in *Nanny McPhee*, *Bright Young Things*, and *A Midsummer Night's Dream*.

DONALD SUTHERLAND

Paths of Glory. It's just a perfect film, and so is *La Strada.* I saw both of them on the same day. They effectively changed my life. They catalyzed certain thoughts that were in my mind. I should say a film can't change your life, but it can cause a change in your life. You must change your own life. Both films are still very clear. They're strong statements about inhumanity as opposed to cruelty. Inhumanity is a far worse emotion.

PATHS OF GLORY (1957). Considered by many to be the quintessential antiwar story due to its emphasis on the insanity of war, this Stanley Kubrick–directed classic stars Kirk Douglas as the commander of a World War I French army troupe whose men refuse to engage in a futile attack. Three of the men are executed for failing to support their general's glory-seeking orders, and it falls to Douglas to defend their decision.

LA STRADA (1954). Master director Federico Fellini took home the best foreign-language film Oscar for this tragic love story between a little clown (Fellini's real-life wife, Giulietta Masina) and a strongman (Anthony Quinn) to whom she is sold. The soulful gaze of Masina permeates the film as the cruel strongman mistreats his gentle companion. The screenplay also received an Oscar nomination.

Tall, distinguished, and always the gentleman, **DONALD SUTHERLAND** came to Hollywood in the late 1960s after studying at London's Academy of Music and Dramatic Arts and then doing small roles in

European horror films. His early films include *The Dirty Dozen* and Robert Altman's masterpiece *M*A*S*H*, where he originated the role of surgeon Hawkeye Pierce. Sutherland went on to star in *Klute, Don't Look Now, Dry White Season, The Day of the Locust, Ordinary People, Eye of the Needle, JFK, Cold Mountain*, and TV's *Commander in Chief*. He stays home one night a week to watch his actor-son Kiefer Sutherland emote on the hit series *24*.

TILDA SWINTON

Oh, there are a million favorites of all time. Off the top of my head, I'd say *A Matter of Life and Death* by Michael Powell and Emeric Pressburger. I thought of this movie while creating the White Witch character for *The Chronicles of Narnia*. The film creates a magical world. *A Matter of Life and Death* is about the fantasy of heaven in a man's mind.

I also knew Michael Powell. I remember him once saying to me, "What film did you see on the plane?" I told him it was *Batman*. He said, "Did you like it?" I replied, "I really didn't like it." He said, "You're wrong. It's a good film." "Why?" I asked him. He replied, "Because it creates its own world and any film that does that is a good film." Michael actually changed my mind about that film, and he was right.

A MATTER OF LIFE AND DEATH (1948). This film by Michael Powell and Emeric Pressburger stars David Niven as a British squadron leader who survives a burning plane and a damaged parachute by landing in the sea during World War II. Because there was a mistake made in heaven, the man has to argue for his life—and his love for a woman he met on radio contact—before a divine court.

London native **TILDA SWINTON** studied at Cambridge University and then at the Royal Shakespeare Company. Her breakthrough role was starring in Sally Potter's *Orlando*. Other films include *Female Perversions*; *Conceiving Ada*; *Love Is the Devil*; *Study for a Portrait of Francis Bacon*; *The Deep End*; *The Beach*; *Vanilla Sky*; *Constantine*; *Broken Flowers*; and *The Chronicles of Narnia: The Lion, the Witch and the Wardrobe*.

WANDA SYKES

For me, the best film is *Dr. Strangelove*. I'm a big Peter Sellers fan. And I just love how that movie is so smart. Look at the time period—the 1960s when it was shot. It was so far ahead of its time. You can still look at this film, which is over forty years old, and consider it a treat. And the film never seems to go away which is proof positive that the movie matters to all the generations. I love the part when they say, "There's no fighting in the war room." That line makes me laugh every single time. And I can't get past the idea that I want to hang out with Peter. Peter was an interesting guy.

DR. STRANGELOVE OR: HOW I LEARNED TO STOP WORRYING AND LOVE THE BOMB (1964). Considered one of Stanley Kubrick's masterworks, this Cold War black comedy stars Peter Sellers as three men attempting to avert a nuclear disaster engineered by a mad U.S. Air Force colonel (Sterling Hayden). It's Sellers who plays an Adlai Stevenson–type U.S. president, a British captain, and the ex-Nazi Strangelove. It's a potent intellectual jab at the absurdity of war and the men who make it, earning Sellers, Kubrick, the film, and its screenplay Oscar nominations.

WANDA SYKES has been called one of the funniest stand-up comedians in America. She grew up in Maryland and began her stand-up career in Washington, D.C. For five years she was a cast member of the HBO hit *The Chris Rock Show*, where she doubled as a performer and writer. The work earned her a writing Emmy. Movie roles have included stints in *Pootie Tang, Nutty Professor II: The Klumps, Down to Earth, Monster-in-Law,* and *Over the Hedge.* Sykes also starred in her TV series, *Wanda at Large,* and wrote and starred in Comedy Central's *Wanda Sykes: Tongue Untied.* She has a regular role on HBO's *Curb Your Enthusiasm.*

LARENZ TATE

I'm going to pick a comedy. I love this movie with Sidney Poitier. Call it blaxploitation. Call it funny. I just call it *Uptown Saturday Night*. I watch that movie all the time. These guys are just really funny to me. Here it is you have two con men—Sidney and Bill Cosby—who will do anything for a buck. Sidney is brilliant and Bill is at his best. The movie also had so many different types of characters coming in and out.

Why don't they make good comedies like this anymore? I love this one because it's full of seasoned actors who come in and out of the film. You can't help but have a good time. This movie was also a platform for these guys to have so much fun. You can see it on their faces.

Like I said, I watch this movie over and over again. I even like the clothes they wear. I appreciate that Bill would do anything for a laugh. And I'm the biggest Sidney fan in history.

UPTOWN SATURDAY NIGHT (1974). Sidney Poitier and Bill Cosby head an all-star cast, including Harry Belafonte, Richard Pryor, and Flip Wilson, as a pair of friends who go to an illegal nightclub. There's a robbery, and inside one of the stolen wallets is a winning lottery ticket that belongs to Poitier. They spend the rest of the film trying to get it back. Poitier did double-duty on the comedy, also serving as director.

LARENZ TATE played Peter in the Oscar-winning best picture *Crash*. He hails from Chicago and has achieved success playing real-life legends Frankie Lymon in *Why Do Fools Fall in Love* and Quincy Jones in *Ray*. He got his start on episodic TV's *21 Jump Street* and *The Wonder Years*. He also starred on the big screen in *Menace II Society*, *The Inkwell*, *Dead Presidents*, *Love Jones*, *The Postman*, *Love Come Down*, *Biker Boyz*, and *A Man Apart*. He runs the production company Tate Men Entertainment with his brothers, writer-producer Larron and actor Lahmard.

CHARLIZE THERON

This morning I was watching *I Could Go on Singing*. It is the best movie I've ever seen. Why? Because when a movie is on at seven in the morning, and you're up intently watching it, then you know it must be a good movie. Frankly, I'd rather be sleeping at that hour. But that's not the point. The point is that you see that this movie is on and you watch no matter what time it is—day or night. Oh, why do I like it so much? It's a movie about a girl who steals the boy. Oh, it just kills me. So good, so good! It's my favorite film of all time. Forget saying I was watching it at seven o'clock this morning and she steals the boy and oh it just kills me. It's my favorite film of all time.

I COULD GO ON SINGING (1963). Judy Garland and Dirk Bogarde slug it out—verbally—as a famed singer and her ex in scenes that seem more improvised than scripted. It's a raw, dramatic film in which the two fight for their son's love while the singer (Garland) is in London for an appearance at the Palladium.

Raised on a farm in South Africa, **CHARLIZE THERON** began emoting as a child who put on shows in the fields for the cows. As a teenager, she was an accomplished ballet dancer who was hired in the United States by the Joffrey Ballet. A knee injury sidelined her dancing career, and Theron opted to dabble in modeling. At eighteen, she was living in Los Angeles and at a local bank trying to cash a check for five hundred dollars. The teller gave her a hard time, and as the story goes, Theron was approached by a man saying he was a show biz manager. It wasn't a come-on line but the beginning of her career. Theron starred in *2 Days in the Valley*, *That Thing You Do!*, *Mighty Joe Young*, *The Astronaut's Wife*, *The Cider House Rules*, *The Yards*, *Sweet November*, and *The Italian Job*. She won a best actress Oscar for playing real-life hooker-turned-killer Aileen Wuornos in *Monster* and was nominated for another Oscar for her recent turn as a female coal miner in *North Country*.

UMA THURMAN

All my life I wanted to work with Meryl Streep, and all my life I wanted to be Doris Day. Well, I worked with Meryl Streep in the movie *Prime*. And I can't be Doris Day, but I can enjoy her movies forever. One of my favorites with Doris is *Pillow Talk*. It's a light, breezy romp of a film that's so much fun to watch. And that bathtub split-screen scene. It's an all-time classic.

I love that Doris didn't play anyone but herself in her movies, like that one, and it was great. You wanted Doris to be Doris. She was just so full of energy and gorgeous. She sang. She danced. She was in those gorgeous A-line dresses. She epitomized a time period and always makes me smile.

PILLOW TALK (1959). Rock Hudson and Doris Day were perfect onscreen lovers, as witnessed in this romantic comedy about a man and woman who hate each other but share a telephone line. He decides to woo her by disguising his voice and romance ensues. The movie won an Oscar for its original screenplay but lost out in the categories of best actress (Day), supporting actress (Thelma Ritter), art direction, and music.

Tough and tender screen beauty **UMA THURMAN** can go by only one name. She grew up in Massachusetts, but left boarding school as a teenager in order to become an actress. She made her screen debut as Cecile de Volanges in *Dangerous Liaisons* and followed up with roles in *Henry & June* and *Pulp Fiction*, which earned her a best supporting actress Oscar nomination. She has also starred in *The Truth About Cats & Dogs*, *Beautiful Girls*, *Gattaca*, *Batman & Robin*, *The Avengers*, and *Sweet and Lowdown*. Thurman proved she was tougher than the rest when she joined forces again with her *Pulp Fiction* director, Quentin Tarantino, for the hit films *Kill Bill: Vol. 1* and *Kill Bill: Vol. 2*.

ROBERT TOWNE

I love *Grand Illusion*. Its theme is magnificent, and it's so beautifully delivered. It's the last moment on earth for these characters. To think there is anything romantic about war—absurd! It's about these two aristocrats on opposite sides—a Frenchman and a German. They know they're relics of the past, regardless of who wins the war and regardless of where it ends. There is the emergence of the bourgeois as evidenced by a young Frenchman and Rosenthal, the Jewish fellow. There is prejudice. But these are the people who are going to be the future. There is a poignancy and beauty to it. I can immerse myself in that world.

I love *Casablanca*. It's one of the most romantic American movies ever made. This is one of the greatest and most entertaining movies ever made. It's virtually set in one setting, but there are a variety of characters and a richness of characters. There is a kind of absolute perfection in the wit of the screenwriters of the 1940s. They could come up with the words.

Then you have the pairing of Bogart and Bergman. It's one of the most brilliant teamings of all time.

I love *Four Feathers*. The hero refuses his commission and his commanding officer says, "I thought I'd never see the day when you're the coward. Go lay down in a dark room and you'll be fine in the morning." Great line. It just throws you back.

THE GRAND ILLUSION (1937). Jean Renoir's classic was nominated for best picture for its depiction of the experiences of two French officers in World War I who are taken prisoner, escape, and reunite in a fortress that is decidedly unfriendly to the lieutenant from an average background and the Jewish prisoner he befriends.

CASABLANCA (1942). The tagline said it all: "They had a date with fate in Casablanca!" Of all of the gin joints in this world, Humphrey Bogart had to step into one in occupied Africa during World War II, where he happens to meet Ilsa Lund, played by Ingrid Bergman. It's the beginning of a beautiful, albeit much too short, romance. Line to love: "Louie, I think this is the beginning of a beautiful friendship."

FOUR FEATHERS (1915). J. Searle Dawley's silent classic has had five adaptations from the A. E. W. Mason novel about a British officer who resigns his post on the eve of his regiment's leaving to battle rebels in 1898 Sudan. Although he plans to regain his honor with a secret undercover assignment, the man is thought to be a coward by everyone, from his fiancée and friends to his fellow officers.

••••••••••••••••••••••••••••••••••

Legendary screenwriter, producer, and director **ROBERT TOWNE** hails from Los Angeles. As a screenwriter, he got his start writing for legendary director Roger Corman and broke into the business with *Last Woman on Earth*. As a script doctor, he wrote key scenes for *Bonnie and Clyde*, *The Godfather*, and *Drive, He Said*. Towne became one of the screenwriters of the 1970s and 1980s by penning *The Last Detail*, *The Parallax View*, *Chinatown*, *Shampoo*, and *Personal Best*. He was so upset with what became of *Greystoke: The Legend of Tarzan, Lord of the Apes* that he had his credit changed to P. H. Vazak, the name of his sheepdog. Towne has also written the scripts for *Tequila Sunrise*, *Days of Thunder*, *The Two Jakes*, *The Firm*, and *Love Affair*. He directed *Personal Best*, *Tequila Sunrise*, *Without Limits*, and *Ask the Dust*. In recent years, he has penned the scripts for *Mission: Impossible*, *Without Limits*, and *Mission: Impossible II*.

BLAIR UNDERWOOD

For me there is a tie between *To Sir, with Love* and *The Exorcist*.

I'm saying *To Sir, with Love* because of Sidney Poitier and his presence and what he represented. I love how he taught those children. He was a great motivator, because you watch how he completely transforms those kids. It's a great film that even set the standard for all the other teacher movies like *Glory Road* or *Remember the Titans*. I love a movie where a teacher comes in to save the day or transform the team. It's just so uplifting to me, because I credit a lot of what happened to me in life from having great teachers.

Now, let's switch gears to my other favorite film, which has to be *The Exorcist*. That film is just one of those great horror movies that just gets under your skin and stays with you. Almost every frame got under my skin. When a film can touch someone like that and make them jump out of their seats, well, then, that film has really done its job. Memorable? Please. I can still see the image of that little girl's face. When it spins . . . freaky! It's still freaky! And they didn't have that much money to do effects in those days, but managed to freak you out.

When Linda Blair crawls backwards, I wanted to hide my eyes. That was just so scary to me. I remember the first time I saw this film, it was on the big screen on Halloween. I walked out just shaking in my boots. Now, I'm not a man who is ever gonna admit to being scared. So in case my wife is reading this, I think we should just write that Blair thinks *The Exorcist* works. Yeah, that's it. It works. Because that sounds more manly.

By the way, I also saw the movie with my wife, and she was scared, so I comforted her. I acted like a man. But I was still shaking in my boots.

....

TO SIR, WITH LOVE (1967). Sidney Poitier stars as a new teacher who has to educate his unruly group of London East End students not only in book knowledge but also in human decency. Pop artist Lulu, who plays one of the students, sings the popular title song.

THE EXORCIST (1973). A twisting head, vomit that looked like pea soup, and a voice that sent chills down the spine figures into William Friedkin's classic thriller about a young girl possessed by demons. Newcomer Linda Blair plays the child opposite Jason Miller and Max von Sydow as the priests who try to cast the demon out. Its chilling score plus an eerie screenplay by William Peter Blatty based on his bestselling novel help make this film one of the most horrifying of all time. Often imitated but never equaled, it won Oscars for Blatty and its sound but lost in the categories of best film, director, actor (Miller), lead actress (Ellen Burstyn), supporting actress (Blair), art direction, cinematography, and editing.

....

Exceptionally handsome and charismatic actor **BLAIR UNDERWOOD** grew up all over the world because his father was in the army. He settled down at Carnegie Mellon to study musical theater and then moved to New York, where he was promptly cast for an episode of *The Cosby Show*. He made a bigger mark for years on *L.A. Law*, where he was called a small-screen Sidney Poitier. His film credits include *Gattaca, Deep Impact, Full Frontal, Just Cause, Asunder*, and HBO's *The Soul of the Game*. He also directed the controversial film *The Second Coming*, in which he played Jesus coming back to earth as an African American.

VINCE VAUGHN

Tender Mercies is a film that I love very much because it's very simple storytelling. His daughter dies, but he doesn't get to go to her death-bed and have any closure. At a moment when he's going to go do something great, record music, he begins to open up and really feel again. He's going to go there with his band. But the phone rings while he's upbeat, and the news comes in that his daughter has been killed.

The man is crippled emotionally in that moment. That's kind of how real life is. You don't have those great closure moments. You get the phone call. Life happens, it flows.

I love that kind of storytelling.

The Bad News Bears is my favorite comedy. I saw that movie as a child, and there was something very real about that movie in that it seemed to be an honest portrayal of people. Matthau is a guy who's really numbing himself. He is obviously a failure in his mind. He isn't accomplishing anything, so he doesn't feel worthy of being loved.

It's not so much that he's mean and doesn't like the kids, but he doesn't feel like he's worth anything. He's a broke-down man and doesn't want to be around. He just wants to numb himself and not feel anything. And this little girl doesn't have a dad and really wants him to be more than what he is. In that movie, he throws a beer in her face. He says, "Can't you get it through your head I don't want to be around you?"

She kind of plays it tough in front of him and you go, *God, why can't they both love each other? Why can't they talk?* He doesn't want to admit that because he doesn't feel that he's worth much. I like those journeys.

....

TENDER MERCIES (1983). Robert Duvall took home an Oscar for his soft-spoken performance as a long-errant country singer who attempts to reconcile with the daughter (Ellen Barkin) he left behind while resurrecting his career. Director Bruce Beresford and his film were nominated as was the film's song "Over You." It also won for Horton Foote's original screenplay.

THE BAD NEWS BEARS (1976). This features Walter Matthau in one of his most famous roles, that of grumpy, aging, ex-minor-league baseball player Morris Buttermaker, who finds himself coaching a group of misfit kids on a California Little League team. Matthau's slow burn and withering looks, not to mention his beer guzzling, make the comedy memorable. And, yes, that's little Tatum O'Neal as one of the players. The film won a Writers Guild of America Award for best original comedy.

....

Charming big lug **VINCE VAUGHN** grew up in suburban Chicago, where he made commercials and his screen debut in *Rudy*. He hit pay dirt with the hip indie film *Swingers*. He has also starred in *The Lost World: Jurassic Park*, *A Cool Dry Place*, *Return to Paradise*, *Clay Pigeons*, a remake of *Psycho*, *The Cell*, *Made*, *Old School*, *Starsky & Hutch*, *Dodgeball: A True Underdog Story*, *Anchorman: The Legend of Ron Burgundy*, *Mr. & Mrs. Smith*, *Wedding Crashers*, and *The Break-Up*.

MARK WAHLBERG

Well, *Taxi Driver* really does it for me. Or maybe I should say Al Pacino in *Dog Day Afternoon*. Or Al Pacino in anything really. I mean, you name it. I feel the same way about John Garfield and Clint Eastwood.

This is so hard, so maybe I'll stick with *Taxi Driver*. I know you want to know why I love it so much. Well, I think that's gonna give you a little too much insight into my own twisted mind! I'm catching on now and saying less and less about myself.

But wait, I'm not leaving it at *Taxi Driver*. I also love *Body and Soul* and *They Made Me a Criminal*.

More than anything, I love everything Jimmy Cagney ever did.

I will give you the "why" about Cagney, although I should be saying less and less about myself. But here goes. Cagney . . . he's like my dad. You know, he's a guy that I can identify with because he's a stand-up guy. He wants to do right. And finally, I like Cagney because of his looks. I don't identify with guys who look better than the girls starring next to them in a movie. Jimmy never had that problem.

....

TAXI DRIVER (1976). Shocking for its time, Martin Scorsese's drama about a crazed New York cabbie (Robert De Niro) infatuated with a political worker (Cybill Shepherd) and a child prostitute (Jodie Foster) won no Oscars despite nominations for best picture, lead actor (De Niro), supporting actress (Foster), and music (Bernard Herrmann).

THEY MADE ME A CRIMINAL (1939). John Garfield teams with The Dead End Kids and director Busby Berkeley in the guilty-pleasure story of a boxer who has a "few too many" and thinks he offed a guy. No wonder the movie comes with the tagline: "I am a fugitive. I am hunted by ruthless men! I am shunned by decent women! I am doomed to hide forever." Poor John. Claude Rains puts in his two cents as Detective Monty Phelan while Ann Sheridan glams it up a bit as Goldie West.

....

MARK WAHLBERG began his career modeling underwear for Calvin Klein and rapping as Marky Mark. But he pulled up his trousers, put down his mike, and opted for an acting career. It was a great move for the Boston native, the youngest of nine children, who got his break from Penny Marshall after she cast him in *Renaissance Man*. Wahlberg hit an acting high note as porn star Dirk Diggler in Paul Thomas Anderson's *Boogie Nights*. He has also starred in *Three Kings, The Perfect Storm, Planet of the Apes, Rock Star, The Truth About Charlie, The Italian Job, Four Brothers,* and *The Departed*. He also produces the hit HBO series *Entourage*.

PAUL WALKER

I want to give you a lofty answer, but I just love *The Big Lebowski*. I can't get enough of the Coen Brothers. And Jeff Bridges as this stoner dude. How can you miss? He's just the ultimate in laid-back cool.

Wait, I can't stop here. I grew up on Harrison Ford, and Indiana Jones remains a role model until today. I just think Dr. Jones is the coolest character ever. He's just awesome. Here you have a super-smart professor who kicks ass. He can wear the spectacles, which make him look like a teacher, but then he tosses on the hat and cracks the whip. He's just the ultimate badass who always got the good-looking girl. Dr. Jones also always lands on his feet. It's not like you think he's going to fall, but still he keeps you on the edge of your seat.

I'm partial to the first Indiana Jones film, which might just be my favorite of all time above *Big Lebowski*. But that could change depending on my mood. Right now I'm remembering the first film, *Raiders of the Lost Ark*. It invited you into this world of Indiana Jones. I'll never forget going to a movie theater as a teenager and watching *Raiders* for the first time. I can hear the music in my head. I can remember the first time you see Harrison Ford. I remember being this kid with this grin on his face. It's that smile you get when in the first few minutes your mind is yelling, *This is going to be a great film!*

Okay, one more. I have three favorites. I'm also partial to *Time Bandits*. Once again, I was a kid when I saw this one. And I loved Sean Connery. I sat there thinking, *I want to be his son*. He was this prince blasting through time with dwarfs and midgets. You can't lose with Sean, dwarfs, and midgets. It was just an awesome ride. I mean, come on. They came face-to-face with Robin Hood. What more do you want in an adventure? That film really takes me back. And then Sean played Harrison's father in an Indiana Jones film, so my friends, we come full circle.

....

THE BIG LEBOWSKI (1998). Here's a typical Joel and Ethan Coen movie, this one about Los Angeles slacker Dude Lebowski (Jeff Bridges) being mistaken for a millionaire of the same name. The poor Lebowski wants some restitution for a rug because a pair of gangsters urinated on it, and, well, that's how a Coen Brothers movie goes.

RAIDERS OF THE LOST ARK (1981). Steven Spielberg put a hat on the head of Harrison Ford and launched a film franchise that got off to an excellent start with four Oscar wins. Ford debuted as rugged archaeologist and adventurer Indiana Jones. In his first adventure, the U.S. government calls upon Dr. Jones to find the Ark of the Covenant before it falls into the hands of the Nazis. Dr. Jones gets a tough-talking love interest in the form of Karen Allen as Marion Ravenwood.

TIME BANDITS (1981). Terry Gilliam directed this movie that came with the tagline "All the dreams you've ever had . . . and not just the good ones." The fantasy film centers on a young boy who teams up with a group of dwarfs who bounce from one time period to the next looking for treasure and spoils. John Cleese shows up as Robin Hood while Sean Connery is King Agamemnon and Ian Holm is Napoleon.

....

Blond and beautiful actor **PAUL WALKER** hails from Glendale, California, and planned on becoming a marine biologist. He got out of the water to become a child actor with roles on *Charles in Charge* and *Who's the Boss?* With his blond surfer-dude looks mixed with brains, he became an A list young actor with starring roles in *Varsity Blues, The Skulls, The Fast and the Furious, Joy Ride, 2 Fast 2 Furious, Timeline, Into the Blue, Running Scared,* and the doggie flick *Eight Below.* He also starred for Clint Eastwood in the World War II epic *Flags of Our Fathers.*

DENZEL WASHINGTON

My favorite film of all time depends on what age I was when I saw it. Films affect you differently during various periods of your life.

But, as a younger man, I really enjoyed *The Education of Sonny Carson*. I just remember that film because it was the first time as a young man that I went to a serious film. I'm the son of a minister, so before that film if I went to the movies, it was a nice film that was pure entertainment. But when I was an older teenager, I heard about this gang film and went to see it.

Here was this film about Sonny and the streets. You get to know Sonny, and then the cops are beating on him. It's completely brutal and shocking.

I just sat there with my eyes wide open thinking, *Wow. Something really serious is going on here.*

I'd be real curious to see the film now. I can't even tell you what the entire movie is about, but it's one of my favorites because it introduced me to the stark reality of the streets.

Of course, I can't leave it at that film. I'll never forget the first time I saw *The Godfather*. It affected me because I remember thinking, *Now, this is a good picture from start to finish.* Otherwise, for pure weirdness in a great way, I loved *Blue Velvet*. It was the first time I saw anything so strange. Suddenly, there's a guy's ear and it's on the ground. You gotta love a movie that has your jaw dropping. At least it provokes a response, which is what a great film is supposed to do for you.

. . . .

THE EDUCATION OF SONNY CARSON (1974). Before *The Shield* or any film by Spike, *Sonny Carson* was known as one of the first films ever to realistically portray gritty, street, gang violence. Set in Brooklyn and starring Rony Clanton, Don Gordon, and Joyce Walker, the grueling film is also known for a climactic funeral scene and a jailhouse moment that predates the reality of the TV series *Oz*. The movie hinges on Sonny's decision to stay with street life or find a new way to exist without the pain.

BLUE VELVET (1986). You can never call director David Lynch mainstream, because here was his simple story of a dark underworld where a young man (Kyle MacLachlan) finds a severed human ear in a field while visiting his hometown. He joins with a police detective's daughter (Laura Dern) to investigate the case. This leads them to a mystery woman (Isabella Rossellini) and her strangely kinky friend (Dennis Hopper), a man who enjoys a whiff of pure oxygen among his other perversities.

. . . .

DENZEL WASHINGTON, dubbed one of *People* magazine's "Sexiest Men Alive," is a native of Mount Vernon, New York, and the son of a Pentecostal minister. He once planned on becoming a journalist and studied writing at Fordham University. A turn in a school play changed his life, and he wound up at the American Conservatory Theater studying theater. He won an Oscar playing a runaway slave named Tripp in *Glory* and is the second African American actor (after Sidney Poitier) to win a best actor Oscar playing a criminal cop in *Training Day*. Washington has also received rave reviews for his roles as Malcolm X, Rubin "Hurricane" Carter, and as a lawyer who takes on the case of an AIDS victim in *Philadelphia*.

KEN WATANABE

Ahhh, a difficult question. I have seen a lot of films, but my favorite remains the old *Romeo and Juliet*. Olivia Hussey is just so beautiful. I was so caught up in the feeling of this love that just couldn't be and these two lovers who died trying to be together. But mostly it was Olivia Hussey. She was the most gorgeous Western girl to me. I saw her the first time as a younger man in this movie, and I just fell in love. She was my Juliet, too.

ROMEO AND JULIET (1968). Leonard Whiting and Olivia Hussey played Shakespeare's tragic lovers in Franco Zeffirelli's lush drama aimed at a youthful audience. He and the film were nominated for Oscars; his cinematographer and costume designer won.

Asian actor **KEN WATANABE** was born in Koide, Niigata, Japan, and grew up with a father who taught calligraphy. At twenty-four, he started to act after the director of England's National Theatre Company informed him that he had "a special gift." Watanabe got his start playing samurai in Japanese movies. He was nominated for a best supporting actor Oscar for acting opposite Tom Cruise in *The Last Samurai*. He also played Ra's al Ghul in *Batman Begins* and starred in *Memoirs of a Geisha*.

FOREST WHITAKER

Does it have to be an American film? I love a really simple film made in China called *Raise the Red Lantern*. It's a very simple movie about the lighting of a candle to show which wife a husband should be with.

It's an amazing film, because it has a physical and a spiritual component to it.

I have two other films that I love. The second is a Sidney Poitier movie called *Brother John*. Sidney plays this mystical guy who comes into this town. He says he'll come with the wind and leave with the wind. This man he plays has seen the end of time. Yet he tries to help this town through a racial event. Will Geer has this great line. He says, "You've seen it? What happens in the end?" That's a question that every person has thought about from time to time in his or her own life.

Finally, I really like *The Fisher King* by Terry Gilliam. Here you have Robin Williams as this guy who is homeless and maybe insane. He actually believes that he's being chased by the red light. There is just something about it that touched me. There is myth behind that film. *The Fisher King* talks about people reclaiming themselves. Jeff Bridges falls from grace and his girlfriend gets killed. Meanwhile, Robin loses his ability to live life. Jeff has lost his life as well and they're both trying to reclaim themselves.

I also love Amanda Plummer as this odd woman.

The film deals with the psychological. Robin keeps losing his mind and feels this horse is chasing him. I like the layer-upon-layer effect of the film. But somehow the whole thing makes some weird sense. I love when Robin climbs this giant skyscraper and steals this cup that he thinks is the Holy Grail.

....

RAISE THE RED LANTERN (1991). When an innocent, nineteen-year-old woman (Gong Li) is forced into marrying a powerful lord who already has three wives, she learns the hard way how to match her rivals' ferocity and claw her way to the top. Directed by Zhang Yimou, the film won the Oscar for best foreign-language film.

BROTHER JOHN (1971). An angel comes down to earth with one question for the people: Is the human race worth saving? The film stars Sidney Poitier, Will Geer, and Beverly Todd.

THE FISHER KING (1991). Jeff Bridges stars as a talk DJ who gives a crazy man advice that prompts a tragedy. Three years later, the guilt-ridden Bridges is saved from being burned to death by a creepy-looking Robin Williams, a street person who demands an unusual payback. In order to repay the favor, the DJ finds himself on a search for the elusive Holy Grail. Terry Gilliam directed the film that saw Mercedes Ruehl take home a best supporting actress Oscar. Williams was nominated for his lead role while other nominations went to the film's screenplay, score, and art direction.

....

FOREST WHITAKER, the soft-spoken character actor with the round face, grew up in Longview, Texas, and graduated from the University of Southern California School of Drama. He cut his teeth in movies such as *Fast Times at Ridgemont High*. Whitaker went on to appear in *Vision Quest*; *Platoon*; *Stakeout*; *Good Morning, Vietnam*; *Bird*; *Johnny Handsome*; *Article 99*; *The Crying Game*; *Blown Away*; *Jason's Lyric*; *Smoke*; and *Phenomenon*. Recent films include *Panic Room* and *Phone Booth*. Whitaker has also stepped behind the camera to direct *Waiting to Exhale*, *Hope Floats*, and *First Daughter*. He just completed a meaty role as an internal affairs detective on the hit cable series *The Shield*.

BRUCE WILLIS

I have a few favorites that I watch in regular rotation. My favorite of all is *Dr. Strangelove*. I love Kubrick, and that film in particular is one of the coolest, funniest, most satirical films ever made, plus it's one of the darkest, too. I love George C. Scott's work in it. His speech when he goes through his five points is just hilarious.

I also love the end speech with Dr. Strangelove and when he's discussing what he can do to keep the human race alive underground. It's just hysterical and just terrific.

DR. STRANGELOVE OR: HOW I LEARNED TO STOP WORRYING AND LOVE THE BOMB (1964). Considered one of Stanley Kubrick's masterworks, this Cold War black comedy stars Peter Sellers as three men attempting to avert a nuclear disaster engineered by a mad U.S. Air Force colonel (Sterling Hayden). It's Sellers who plays an Adlai Stevenson–type U.S. president, a British captain, and the ex-Nazi Strangelove. It's a potent intellectual jab at the absurdity of war and the men who make it, earning Sellers, Kubrick, the film, and its screenplay Oscar nominations.

BRUCE WILLIS, nicknamed "Bruno," was born in Germany on a military base and grew up in Penns Grove, New Jersey. After graduating from high school, he attended Montclair State University in Montclair, New Jersey. He moved to New York to become an actor and became a bartender by night so he could audition during the daylight hours. Pouring drinks paid off, because a casting director wandered into his bar one night and gave him a small role in a movie as . . . a bartender. His big break happened in 1985 when he became wise-cracking detective David Addison on the popular ABC-TV series *Moonlighting*. Willis crossed over to film with the hit *Die Hard* and then *In Country, Die Hard 2, The Bonfire of the Vanities, Hudson Hawk, Pulp Fiction, Color of Night, Nobody's Fool, The Fifth Element, Armageddon, The Sixth Sense, Tears of the Sun, The Whole Ten Yards,* and *Sin City*.

OWEN WILSON

I love *Punch-Drunk Love* and *The Insider*.

With *Punch-Drunk Love*, I loved the story. I thought that was like a great romantic story that didn't make you cringe.

As for *The Insider*, I just found that just really moving. Russell is like an Everyman father sort of thing. There's that scene where he goes running out of the house and he trips and falls. I just found it moving, and I thought that Russell Crowe was great in it.

PUNCH-DRUNK LOVE (2002). Whoever said Adam Sandler can't act never saw him go for broke in Paul Thomas Anderson's disjointed story of a businessman who wants to fall in love but can't seem to, in no small thanks to his seven sisters. Then someone drops a harmonium near his shop, and mysterious Emily Watson enters his life. Anderson won best director honors at the Cannes Film Festival and was nominated for a Golden Palm.

THE INSIDER (1999). Before he was Maximus the gladiator, Russell Crowe was Oscar-nominated for his role as whistleblower Jeffrey Wigand, whose appearance on TV's *60 Minutes* was not aired due to pressure from CBS parent company Westinghouse. Based on a true story involving the tobacco industry, the Michael Mann drama was nominated for best picture, director, actor, cinematography, editing, sound, and adapted screenplay.

Texan **OWEN WILSON** grew up with his brothers Andrew and Luke Wilson. At the University of Texas at Austin, he met his future filmmaking partner, Wes Anderson. They joined together to write the screenplay for the critically acclaimed film *Bottle Rocket*. Early film work includes *The Cable Guy*, *The Haunting*, *Anaconda*, *Breakfast of Champions*, and *Shanghai Noon*. He has also starred in *Meet the Parents*; *Behind Enemy Lines*; *The Royal Tenenbaums*; *The Life Aquatic with Steve Zissou*; *Wedding Crashers*; *The Wendell Baker Story*; and *You, Me and Dupree*.

PATRICK WILSON

It's a given for any boy in the 1970s to love *The Empire Strikes Back*. *The Empire* is the second *Star Wars*. I was waiting and waiting for the sequel, and here was one that didn't disappoint. It was a great and strong sequel. You find out a lot about the characters, and you have that great Luke and Leia kiss.

This is a darker *Star Wars*. I also love that there weren't as many characters running around for comic relief. There weren't silly monsters running around. Much more in on the line here, and I loved that fact. But you still had Harrison Ford, who is the greatest. Han Solo is one of the classics. He is the coolest guy in the galaxy.

STAR WARS: EPISODE V—THE EMPIRE STRIKES BACK (1980). Darth Vader menaces Luke Skywalker's friends in his attempt to get to Luke, who is being trained as a Jedi by Yoda. Vader reveals his relationship to Luke in the film directed by Irwin Kershner and considered one of the strongest in the series. It won an Oscar only for its sound, however, and was bypassed in the categories of art direction and music. A special achievement Oscar for its visual effects was awarded.

Norfolk, Virginia, native **PATRICK WILSON** has a B.F.A. in drama from Carnegie Mellon University and a slew of Broadway hits under his belt, including Tony-nominated roles in *The Full Monty* and *Oklahoma!* Wilson had big screen roles in *The Alamo*, *The Phantom of the Opera*, *Hard Candy*, *Running with Scissors*, and *Little Children*.

REESE WITHERSPOON

Hands down, my favorite movie is *Splendor in the Grass*. I just love Natalie Wood, and I think this is one of her best performances in a movie that breaks my heart each and every time I see it.

How can you not weep at the end, when Deenie, played by Natalie, gets out of that mental institution and goes home engaged to this doctor although she really still loves her high school sweetheart, Bud, played by Warren Beatty. Deenie comes home, puts on her most beautiful and lovely white outfit. And then even though she's engaged to someone else, she drives out with her friends to the farm where Bud is living.

Bud used to be very rich, but his father lost it all in the crash and now he's a poor farmer with all this dirt and sweat on him. Deenie still looks at him lovingly and says a line that just makes me cry. She says, "Bud, are you happy?" And he says, "I don't think about that anymore."

Oh, I just love it. I just hope that Hollywood never ever decides to remake it. You couldn't duplicate that look of tragedy on both the faces of Natalie and Warren. It's all about lost opportunity, and so many of us have been there in real life. They were so much in love and then life intervened. Heartbreaking!

SPLENDOR IN THE GRASS (1961). Natalie Wood and Warren Beatty, in his screen debut, eventually became real-life lovers. But in playwright William Inge's Oscar-winning original screenplay, they played a tragic pair of teenagers whose lives were shattered by the sexual constraints of their time—the late 1920s and early 1930s in rural Kansas. In her Oscar-nominated role, Wood played a high school girl in love with a rich sports hero classmate. Warned by her puritanical mother not to "go all the way" with the boy, she makes a choice that drives her to the edge of madness and changes her life forever. Elia Kazan directed the bittersweet love story that was Inge's first written directly for the screen.

·······································

Oscar winner **REESE WITHERSPOON** took home a little gold statue in 2006 for playing June Carter Cash in *Walk the Line*. The former Laura Jean Reese Witherspoon grew up in Nashville, where she began her career as a model and by doing local TV commercials. She got her film break in 1990 in Robert Mulligan's *The Man on the Moon*, which earned her rave reviews for playing a tomboy who must grow up. Witherspoon has also starred in *Election, Pleasantville, Cruel Intentions, Fear, The Importance of Being Earnest, Legally Blonde, Sweet Home Alabama*, and *Vanity Fair*.

ELIJAH WOOD

I always come back to *Harvey* with Jimmy Stewart. It's a really profound movie, and I gain something new every single time I see it. I love a film about a man who lets go of reality because he's disappointed when he looks at the world around him. His disappointment manifests itself into a giant white rabbit. I see his rabbit character as more of a choice, and it's beautiful.

HARVEY (1950). James Stewart won an Oscar nomination for his role as a drunk who has an unseen friend he calls Harvey. Harvey is a six-foot-three-inch rabbit that no one but Elwood P. Dowd (Stewart) can see, although Elwood's sister (Josephine Hull, who won a best supporting actress Oscar for the role) can see him at times. Sis winds up in a sanatorium by mistake before the doctor in charge goes after Elwood.

A hard Hobbit to break, **ELIJAH WOOD** starred in the Oscar-winning *The Lord of the Rings* trilogy, where he played ring-bearer Frodo Baggins, the little Hobbit who saved all of Middle Earth. The Cedar Rapids, Iowa, native began acting as a child with roles in *Deep Impact*, *The Ice Storm*, *The Good Son*, *Radio Flyer*, and *Avalon*. He has also starred in *Eternal Sunshine of the Spotless Mind*, *Sin City*, and *Bobby*. Wood is the proud owner of one of the two rings used in the *Lord of the Rings* films.

EVAN RACHEL WOOD

I have to be true to myself and say *Labyrinth*. I've been obsessed with that movie since I can remember. I love David Bowie and the songs. I had a huge poster in my room of Bowie when I was a girl.

As for the film, I just love everything about that movie. He was the first person I ever had a crush on. When I was a teenager, I thought, *What is this strange feeling I'm having watching him? And I really like the eyeliner he's* wearing. I just thought he was so cool because he was soooo cool. I was also obsessed with his voice.

I didn't even know he was Bowie when I watched the movie for the first time. Then I went to a record store and saw his CDs. I thought, *Wow, this is the guy from* Labyrinth. *He's a huge star. And he wears those great funky pants!*

LABYRINTH (1986). The late Muppet master Jim Henson directs the fantasy about a girl (Jennifer Connelly) who has sixteen hours to rescue her baby brother from evil Jareth, the Goblin King (David Bowie, aka The Coolest Human Being on Earth).

....

EVAN RACHEL WOOD is one of the most promising actresses of her generation. The fragile-looking blonde with great spirit grew up in Raleigh, North Carolina. She made her mark as a teenage actress in the hit ABC-TV show *Once and Again* where she played young Jessie. On the big screen, she has appeared in *Practical Magic*, opposite Sandra Bullock and Nicole Kidman, *S1m0ne* with Al Pacino, and with Tommy Lee Jones in *The Missing*. Wood has also starred in *Pretty Persuasion*, *The Upside of Anger*, *Running with Scissors*, and the Beatles-based musical *Across the Universe* directed by Julie Taymor.

ALFRE WOODARD

I love Robert Altman, and one of my favorite films of his is 3 *Women*. First of all, it was these wonderful women on the big screen, and they were all very different.

I like the filmmaking, including the tone and the way it was shot.

I also like how the movie didn't explain things, so I could read a lot of things into it. But I also felt like I could be any of those women. It attracted me and disturbed me at the same time.

I love a movie that surprises me. I get tired of being able to chart what time it is in real life by where you are in the movie. Okay, we're at this point, so we only have half an hour left. Okay, the main guy just got the girl so we're at the end. I hate that. I don't like keeping time in movies, because I want to escape and forget real life. 3 *Women* made me forget. The sensibility of that film is to keep you guessing. I couldn't tell time by what was happening on the big screen.

It would be interesting to see it as a grown woman and see it again since now I'm a mom. I saw it the last time fifteen years ago. Wow, that's a long time. I gotta get the DVD.

3 WOMEN (1977). Actresses love director Robert Altman for a reason—he lets them pull out all the stops in colorful roles. Here he directs Sissy Spacek, Shelley Duvall, and Janice Rule in a drama about two women (Spacek and Duvall) who switch personalities at the solarium where they work. Rule plays an artist who wanders around their story.

....

ALFRE WOODARD is an award-winning actress who began her career on Broadway and received an Emmy for her role in HBO's *Miss Evers' Boys* and an ACE Award for playing Winnie Mandela in *Mandela*. Her extensive list of feature films include *The Singing Detective*, *How to Make an American Quilt*, *Passion Fish*, *The Forgotten*, *Crooklyn*, and *Something New*. She is also a cast member of the megahit ABC series *Desperate Housewives*.

CATHERINE ZETA-JONES

This is such an easy one because I love *Breakfast at Tiffany's*. It's a brilliant film that stars the most gorgeous woman ever on the big screen—Audrey Hepburn. Breathtaking. She had such style and class, and remains an inspiration to me. How could you not love this movie which makes you just want to run as fast as you can to beautiful New York?

BREAKFAST AT TIFFANY'S (1961). Truman Capote wrote the novel in part about his real-life friend, Carol, who eventually married Walter Matthau, but it was Audrey Hepburn who got to play Holly Golightly, a New York paid escort looking for a rich man but in love with a struggling writer (George Peppard). The film's wildly popular "Moon River" by Johnny Mercer won an Academy Award, as did Henry Mancini's music. Hepburn was nominated for her lead performance but failed to win. Neither did the nominated screenplay and art direction. Look for Mickey Rooney in the badly miscast and politically incorrect role of a Japanese neighbor.

The beauty from Swansea, Wales, **CATHERINE ZETA-JONES** got her start on stage in *42nd Street* and then on the small screen in England in the saga *The Darling Buds of May*. It's no coincidence that she also starred on the small screen as *Catherine the Great*. Zeta-Jones broke hearts (including that of Michael Douglas, who says it was love at first sight) when she swashbuckled opposite Antonio Banderas in

The Legend of Zorro. She has also starred in *Entrapment*, *Traffic*, *Intolerable Cruelty*, *The Terminal*, and *Ocean's Twelve*. Zeta-Jones won a best supporting actress Oscar for her role as showgirl on death row Velma Kelly in *Chicago*. She is married to Michael Douglas and is the mother of their two children, Dylan and Carys.

ACKNOWLEDGMENTS

Thanks to Joyce Persico for your wisdom, guidance, wonderful film knowledge, late-night phone calls, everlasting friendship, hard work, and dedication.

Thanks to Richard Abate at ICM for the first "Pearlman original." Bigger thanks for your belief in me, amazing guidance over the years, and never-ending support.

Thanks to Kate Lee at ICM for all your help and hard work.

Thanks to David Cashion at Penguin for making this a truly joyful project. I hope it's our first of many together.

Thanks to my friends, including Sally Kline, Vickie Chachere, Amy Longsdorf, Louis B. Hobson, Earl Dittman, and Steven Schaefer for your friendship, support, and laughter. Special thanks to Steven for your amazing knowledge of film and your ability to interrupt in the best possible way.

Thanks to John Barron, Christine Ledbetter, Avis Weathersbee, Darel Jevens, Laura Emerick, Debra Douglas, and Tom Connor at the *Chicago Sun-Times* for your many years of wonderful friendship and support.

Thanks to Gayden Wren at the New York Times Syndicate—an amazing editor.

Thanks to my brother and attorney Gavin M. Pearlman for looking out for me and for your love. Special thanks to Jill Pearlman (a fantastic Mom), my nephews Reid J. Pearlman and Cade Matthew Pearlman, Richard and Cheryl Pearlman (the best aunt and uncle in the world), Kim and Jason Pearlman, and Beth Ann and Craig Pearlman.

To Jake and Cody—the best assistants on four legs each.

Thanks to my father, Paul Pearlman, for being my biggest supporter and for your love.

Thanks to Michael Drapp for the ultimate love story.

INDEX

Ace in the Hole, 44–45
Addy, Mark, 120
Affleck, Ben, 177, 178
All That Jazz, 24
Allen, Joan, 1–2, 113
Allen, Karen, 225
Allen, Tim, 3
Allen, Woody, 64, 130, 177
Almodóvar, Pedro, 1
Altman, Robert, 4–5, 241
Ameche, Don, 182
*Anchorman: The Legend of Ron
    Burgundy*, 119
Anderson, Anthony, 6–7
Anderson, Paul Thomas, 233
Anderson, Wes, 84
Andersson, Bibi, 4
Andrews, Dana, 147
Andrews, Julie, 15, 16, 28
Andrews, Naveen, 8
Angel and the Badman, 114, 115
Aniston, Jennifer, 9–10
Ann-Margret, 140
Annie Hall, 64, 130
Antonioni, Michelangelo, 90
Apartment, The, 57–58
Apollonia, 72
Applegate, Christina, 119
Arabian Nights, 155
Arkin, Alan, 183
Arletty, 138
Armstrong, Robert, 111

Ashby, Hal, 170, 175, 192
Astaire, Fred, 149
Avildsen, John G., 7, 185
Aykroyd, Dan, 77, 181
Aznavour, Charles, 54

Bacon, Kevin, 66
Bad News Bears, The, 220, 221
Bad Sleep Well, The, 11–12
Badham, John, 167
Badham, Mary, 151
Bailey, Fenton, 15–16
Baker, Joe Don, 97
Baldwin, Alec, 183
Ballard, Carol, 11–12
Bancroft, Anne, 203
Banderas, Antonio, 13–14
Barbato, Randy, 15–16
Barkin, Ellen, 221
Barrault, Jean-Louis, 138
Barrymore, Drew, 199
Baxter, Anne, 14
Beatty, Warren, 169, 236
Becker, Howard, 124
Begley, Ed, 62, 172
Being There, 175, 192
Belafonte, Harry, 210
Bellamy, Ralph, 182
Belushi, Jim, 77
Belushi, John, 77
Benchley, Peter, 76
Beresford, Bruce, 139, 221

Bergman, Ingmar, 4, 41
Bergman, Ingrid, 106, 107, 188, 216, 217
Berkeley, Busby, 222
Bernstein, Elmer, 147, 151
Bernstein, Leonard, 36, 52, 62
Beymer, Richard, 143
Bicycle Thief, The, 177, 178
Big Lebowski, The, 99–100, 224, 225
Birch, Thora, 79
Black, Jack, 17–18
Blacula, 123, 124
Blair, Linda, 218, 219
Blatty, William Peter, 219
Blethyn, Brenda, 19–20
Bloom, Orlando, 179
Blue Velvet, 226, 227
Blues Brothers, The, 77
Body and Soul, 222
Bogarde, Dirk, 212
Bogart, Humphrey, 52, 106, 107, 188, 216, 217
Bolger, Ray, 55, 129, 189
Bowie, David, 145, 239
Bracco, Lorraine, 40, 173, 174
Bradley, David, 51
Brando, Marlon, 36, 46, 51–52, 62, 92, 199
"Breaker" Morant, 138, 139
Breakfast at Tiffany's, 243
Brent, George, 187
Breslin, Spencer, 21–22
Brickman, Marshall, 64, 130
Bridge on the River Kwai, The, 173
Bridges, Jeff, 99, 103, 224, 225, 229, 230
Brief Encounter, 4
Bring Me the Head of Alfredo Garcia, 114, 115
Broderick, Matthew, 158
Brody, Adrien, 23
Bronson, Charles, 147
Brooks, James L., 9, 24, 116, 132
Brother John, 229, 230
Brown, Bryan, 138, 139
Bryant, Joy, 25

Brynner, Yul, 147
Burstyn, Ellen, 219
Butch Cassidy and the Sundance Kid, 181–182
Bye Bye Birdie, 140

Caan, James, 199
Cabaret, 156
Cabot, Bruce, 111
Cagney, James, 197, 222
Calamity Jane, 19
Candy, John, 39, 40, 77
Capote, Truman, 243
Capra, Frank, 94
Carell, Steve, 119
Carné, Marcel, 138
Carrey, Jim, 26–27
Carroll, Diahann, 123, 124, 162
Carter, Helena Bonham, 28–29, 43
Casablanca, 106, 107, 188, 216, 217
Cassavetes, John, 163
Cattaneo, Peter, 119
Cazale, John, 2, 199
Cedric the Entertainer, 30–31
Chakiris, George, 143
Chaplin, Charlie, 186
Chapman, Graham, 99
Chariots of Fire, 61, 62
Charleson, Ian, 61
Chayefsky, Paddy, 26
Children of Paradise, 138–139
Chinatown, 70–71
Chitty Chitty Bang Bang, 153–154
Cimino, Michael, 1
Citizen Kane, 66, 186
Clanton, Rony, 227
Clarke, Arthur C., 21
Claudine, 123, 124, 162
Cleese, John, 99, 225
Clooney, George, 32–33
Cobb, Lee J., 36, 52, 62, 172
Coen Brothers, 99, 224, 225
Cohen, Rob, 34–35
Cohn, Nik, 167
Columbus, Chris, 36–37, 180
Connelly, Jennifer, 145, 239

Connery, Sean, 224–225
Cook, Dane, 39–40
Cook, Rachel Leigh, 38
Cool Hand Luke, 97
Cooley High, 6, 7
Cooper, Gary, 146
Cooper, Merian C., 111
Coppola, Francis Ford, 46, 84, 134, 199
Cort, Bud, 170
Cosby, Bill, 210
Costa-Gavras, Constantin, 88, 89
Cotten, Joseph, 14
Cowell, Simon, 15–16
Crawford, Joan, 107
Cronenberg, David, 41–42
Cross, Ben, 62
Crowe, Cameron, 38, 96
Crowe, Russell, 233
Cruise, Tom, 66, 124
Cukor, George, 57
Curtis, Jamie Lee, 182
Curtiz, Michael, 188
Cusack, John, 38, 96
Cuthbert, Elisha, 43

Dafoe, Willem, 8
Dahl, John, 44–45
Dahl, Roald, 154
Damon, Matt, 46–47, 177, 178
Daniels, Jeff, 10, 74–76, 117, 132
Dark Victory, 187
Davis, Bette, 107, 187
Davis, Kristin, 48–49
Dawley, J. Searle, 217
Day, Doris, 19, 125, 126, 214
Day, Morris, 72
Day-Lewis, Daniel, 50–52
De Havilland, Olivia, 60, 67, 127
De Niro, Robert, 1, 23, 40, 46, 50, 51,
    130, 131, 134, 173, 174, 183, 184,
    222
De Palma, Brian, 30
De Sica, Vittorio, 178
De Vito, Danny, 10, 117, 132
Dead Poets Society, The, 6
Deer Hunter, The, 1–2

Demme, Jonathan, 53–54, 74, 76
Depp, Johnny, 55–56, 101, 152
Dern, Laura, 227
Deschanel, Zooey, 57–58
DiCaprio, Leonardo, 197
Diesel, Vin, 59–60
Dietrich, Marlene, 14
*Dr. Strangelove or: How I Learned to
    Stop Worrying and Love the Bomb*,
    21, 32, 112–113, 208, 231
Dog Day Afternoon, 222
Donen, Stanley, 148
Douglas, Jerry, 61–63
Douglas, Kirk, 44, 204
Douglas, Melvyn, 175, 192
Dourif, Brad, 17
Dreams, 114
Drescher, Fran, 64–65
Dreyer, Theodor, 165, 166
Dreyfuss, Richard, 66–67
Driver, Minnie, 68–69, 178
Duchovny, David, 70–71
Dujmovic, Davor, 192
Dukakis, Olympia, 160
Dunaway, Faye, 26, 70, 71
Durning, Charles, 68
Duvall, Robert, 51, 150, 221
Duvall, Shelley, 241

Education of Sonny Carson, The, 226,
    227
Ekberg, Anita, 41
Elise, Kimberly, 72–73
Elk, 118
English Patient, The, 108
E.T. The Extra-Terrestrial, 199
Exorcist, The, 218, 219

Fail-Safe, 32, 33
Falconetti, Maria, 165, 166
Farrelly, Bobby, 74–76
Farrelly, Peter, 74–76
Farrow, Mia, 163–164
Fast Times at Ridgemont High, 6, 7
Favreau, Jon, 77–78
Fellini, Federico, 41, 204

Ferrell, Will, 118, 119
Ferrera, America, 79–80
Ferris Bueller's Day Off, 158
Few Good Men, A, 66
Field, Sally, 160
50 Cent (Curtis Jackson), 81
Fight Club, 43
Finch, Peter, 26
Fincher, David, 43
Finding Neverland, 106
Fisher, Carrie, 77
Fisher King, The, 103, 229, 230
Fitzgerald, Geraldine, 126
Fleming, Ian, 154
Fleming, Victor, 59, 67
Fletcher, Louise, 17
Fonda, Henry, 33, 61, 62, 146, 147, 172
Foner, Naomi, 82–83
Foote, Horton, 151, 221
Ford, Harrison, 136, 224, 225, 235
Forman, Milos, 17
48 Hours, 181, 182
Fosse, Bob, 24, 156
Foster, Jodie, 23, 174, 222
Four Feathers, 216, 217
Foxx, Jamie, 6
Franco, James, 84–85
Freeman, Morgan, 7, 86–87, 150–151
Friday, 81
Friedkin, William, 219
From Here to Eternity, 50
Full Monty, The, 119–120
Funny Face, 148, 149

Gable, Clark, 59, 60, 67
Gaghan, Stephen, 88–89
Garfield, John, 222
Garland, Judy, 55, 129, 148, 189, 212
Garr, Teri, 68
Gazzo, Michael V., 46, 134
Geer, Will, 229, 230
Gere, Richard, 90–91
Gilliam, Terry, 92–93, 99, 103, 225, 229, 230
Glengarry Glen Ross, 183
Godfather, The, 199, 226

Godfather: The, Part II, 46, 134
Goldsmith, Akiva, 94–95
Gone With the Wind, 59–60, 66, 67
Gong Li, 230
Good Morning, Vietnam, 6
Good Will Hunting, 177, 178
Goodfellas, 39–40, 173–174, 196
Goodis, David, 53
Gordon, Don, 227
Gordon, Ruth, 97, 163, 170
Gorney, Karen, 167
Graduate, The, 203
Grand Illusion, 216–217
Grant, Cary, 57
Grant, Hugh, 108
Great Dictator, The, 186
Great Escape, The, 153
Great Expectations (1946), 194
Grey, Joel, 156
Griffith, Melanie, 74–76, 79
Grizzly Man, 190
Groundhog Day, 48
Guiness, Alec, 136

Hackman, Gene, 25
Hagen, Jean, 148
Haley, Jack, 55, 129, 189
Hall, Jon, 155
Hamill, Mark, 136
Hamlisch, Marvin, 100
Hanks, Tom, 6
Hannah, Daryl, 6, 160
Hannigan, Alyson, 96
Harling, Robert, 160
Harlow, Jean, 197
Harold and Maude, 32, 97, 169, 170
Harrelson, Woody, 97–98
Harris, Ed, 183
Harry Potter and the Sorcerer's Stone, 179–180
Hartnett, Josh, 99–100
Harvey, 121–122, 238
Hawks, Howard, 196, 197
Hayden, Sterling, 112, 208, 231
Hayek, Selma, 101–102

Head, Edith, 52
Heat, 183, 184
Heckerling, Amy, 7
Heder, Jon, 53
Henson, Jim, 145, 239
Hepburn, Audrey, 51, 52, 149, 243
Hepburn, Katharine, 57, 125, 126
Herrmann, Bernard, 23, 174, 222
Hershey, Barbara, 8
Herzog, Werner, 190
Hess, Jared, 53
Heston, Charlton, 13
Hill, George Roy, 100, 181
Hilton-Jacobs, Lawrence, 7
Hobson, Valerie, 194
Hobson's Choice, 50, 51
Hoffman, Dustin, 68, 203
Hoffmann, Gaby, 79
Holden, William, 26, 52
Holm, Ian, 62, 225
Holt, Tim, 14
Hopper, Dennis, 97, 227
Houston, Dianne, 103
Howard, Terrence, 104–105
Howard, Trevor, 4
Hudson, Hugh, 62
Hudson, Kate, 106–107
Hudson, Rock, 126, 214
Huffman, Felicity, 108–109
Hughes, John, 40, 158
Hull, Josephine, 121, 238
Hunt, Martita, 194
Hunter, Ian McLellan, 52
Hussey, Olivia, 228
Hussey, Ruth, 57
Huston, Anjelica, 25
Huston, John, 70
Hutton, Timothy, 124

I Could Go on Singing, 212
Ice Cube, 81
Idle, Eric, 99
Inge, William, 169, 236
Insider, The, 233
It's a Wonderful Life, 94

Jackson, Peter, 110–111, 180
Jarre, Maurice, 34, 171
Jaws, 75
Jeffries, Lionel, 154
Jet Li, 136–137
Johnson, Celia, 4
Johnson, Tim, 112–113
Jones, James Earl, 124, 162
Jones, Jeffrey, 158
Jones, Terry, 99
Jones, Tommy Lee, 114–115
Judd, Ashley, 184
Jules and Jim, 82
Jungle Book, The, 121

Karloff, Boris, 197
Kazan, Elia, 36, 51, 62, 169, 237
Keaton, Diane, 64, 130, 199
Keel, Howard, 19
Keitel, Harvey, 51, 131
Kelly, Gene, 148
Kennedy, George, 97
Kershner, Irwin, 235
Kes, 50, 51
Kidman, Nicole, 86, 116–117
Kilcher, Q' Orianka, 118
Kilmer, Val, 104, 119–120, 184
King, Stephen, 151
King Kong (1933), 110, 111
Kingsley, Ben, 113
Kitten with a Whip, 140
Klein, Chris, 121–122
Klugman, Jack, 62, 172
Kristofferson, Kris, 115
Kruschen, Jack, 58
Kubrick, Stanley, 21, 22, 32, 112, 204, 208, 231
Kurosawa, Akira, 3, 11, 12, 114, 147, 201
Kusturica, Emir, 192

La Dolce vita, 41
La Strada, 204
Labyrinth, 145, 239
Lahr, Bert, 55, 129, 189
Landis, John, 77

Lange, Jessica, 24, 68
Last Temptation of Christ, The, 8
Lathan, Sanaa, 125–126
Latifah, Queen, 123–124
Laughton, Charles, 50, 51
Lawrence of Arabia, 34, 134, 171
Leachman, Cloris, 79, 127–128
Lean, David, 34, 51, 171, 194
Lean on Me, 6, 7
Ledger, Heath, 129
Lee, Ang, 108
Lee, Harper, 151
Leguizamo, John, 86, 130–131
Leigh, Janet, 13
Leigh, Jennifer Jason, 7
Leigh, Vivien, 59, 67
Lemmon, Jack, 5, 183
Leoni, Téa, 132–133
Levy, Eugene, 134–135
Lindo, Delroy, 138–139
Liotta, Ray, 40, 74–76, 173, 174
Lithgow, John, 10, 117, 132
Loach, Ken, 51
Lohan, Lindsay, 140–141
London, Michael, 142
Lopez, Jennifer, 143–144
Lord of the Flies, 123
*Lord of the Rings, The: The Fellowship
     of the Ring*, 180
Low Down Dirty Shame, A, 30
Lucas, George, 136
Lumet, Sidney, 32, 33, 62, 172
Lynch, David, 227

MacDowell, Andie, 48
MacLachan, Kyle, 227
MacLaine, Shirley, 9, 58, 116, 132, 160
MacMurray, Fred, 57
Magnificent Ambersons, The, 13, 14
Magnificent Seven, The, 146, 147, 201
Mahoney, John, 38
Malden, Karl, 36, 52, 62, 92
Malkovich, John, 96
Malone, Jena, 145
Man for All Seasons, A, 50
Mancini, Henry, 243

Mankiewicz, Herman J., 66
Mann, Michael, 184, 233
Mantegna, Joe, 113
Marshall, E. G., 62, 172
Marshall, Garry, 146–147
Marshall, Rob, 148–149
Marshall, William, 124
Martin, Jesse L., 150–151
Martin, Steve, 39, 40
Martin, Strother, 97
Mary Poppins, 28
Masina, Giulietta, 204
Mastroianni, Marcello, 41
Matter of Life and Death, A, 206
Matthau, Walter, 220, 221, 243
McAdams, Rachel, 152
McDaniel, Hattie, 60, 67
McGregor, Ewan, 86
McGuigan, Paul, 153–154
McKellen, Ian, 180
McQueen, Steve, 147
Mean Streets, 50, 51, 130–131
Meet Me in St. Louis, 148
Meirelles, Fernando, 155
Mercer, Johnny, 243
Meredith, Burgess, 185
Meron, Neil, 156–157
Merriman, Ryan, 158–159
Mifune, Toshirô, 3, 12, 201
Miller, Jason, 219
Mills, John, 194
Minnelli, Liza, 156
Mitchell, Margaret, 59, 67
Mitchum, Robert, 112, 113, 142
Monaghan, Michelle, 160–161
Mo'nique, 162
Monroe, Marilyn, 140
Montez, Maria, 155
Monty Python and the Holy Grail, 99
Moore, Ashleigh Aston, 79
Moore, Demi, 66, 79
Moore, Julianne, 163–164
Moorehead, Agnes, 14
Moreau, Jeanne, 82
Moreno, Rita, 143
Mortensen, Viggo, 165–166, 179

Mortimer, Emily, 167–168
Moulin Rouge!, 86
Mulligan, Robert, 151
Muni, Paul, 196, 197
Murphy, Eddie, 181, 182
Murray, Bill, 48, 68, 84

Napoleon Dynamite, 53
Network, 26
Newman, Paul, 97, 99, 100, 182
Niagara, 140
Nichols, Mike, 203
Nicholson, Jack, 9, 10, 17, 66, 70, 71, 90, 106, 116, 117, 132
Niven, David, 206
Nolte, Nick, 182
Norma Rae, 97
Norton, Edward, 43
Now and Then, 79

Oates, Warren, 115
Oberon, Merle, 125
O'Brien, Margaret, 148
O'Connor, Donald, 148
O'Donnell, Rosie, 79
Oliver!, 153
Olivier, Laurence, 125
On the Waterfront, 36, 51–52, 61, 62
One-Eyed Jacks, 92
One Flew Over the Cuckoo's Nest, 17
O'Neal, Tatum, 221
O'Toole, Peter, 34, 171
Out of the Past, 112, 113, 142
Ox-Bow Incident, The, 146, 147

Pacino, Al, 30, 46, 134, 183, 184, 199, 222
Palin, Michael, 99
Palmer, Leland, 24
Paltrow, Gwyneth, 25
Parton, Dolly, 160
Passenger, The, 90
Passion de Jeanne d'Arc, La, 165–166
Paths of Glory, 204
Paxton, Bill, 169–170
Pearson, Jesse, 140

Peck, Gregory, 52, 151
Peckinpah, Sam, 114, 115
Penn, Sean, 6, 7, 126
Peppard, George, 243
Persona, 4
Pesci, Joe, 40, 174
Pfeiffer, Michelle, 30
Philadelphia Story, The, 57
Pickens, Slim, 92
Pillow Talk, 125, 126, 214
Pinter, Harold, 91
Pitt, Brad, 43
Planes, Trains & Automobiles, 39, 40
Plummer, Amanda, 229
Plummer, Christopher, 16
Poitier, Sidney, 210, 218, 219, 229, 230
Polanski, Roman, 70, 71, 163, 164
Pollack, Sydney, 68
Pomeranc, Max, 113
Portman, Natalie, 184
Powell, Michael, 206
Pressburger, Emeric, 206
Pretty Woman, 140
Pride of the Yankees, The, 146–147
Prince, 72
Pryce, Jonathan, 183
Pryor, Richard, 210
Public Enemy, 197
Punch-Drunk Love, 233
Purple Rain, 72

Quaid, Dennis, 171
Quinn, Anthony, 147, 204

Radcliffe, Daniel, 172
Raft, George, 196, 197
Raging Bull, 50
Raiders of the Lost Ark, 224, 225
Rains, Claude, 223
Raise the Red Lantern, 229, 230
Ramis, Harold, 48, 173–174
Ratner, Brett, 175–176
Ray, 6
Redford, Robert, 100, 181
Reiner, Rob, 66
Reinking, Ann, 24

Renoir, Jean, 216
Reynolds, Debbie, 148
Rhys Meyers, Jonathan, 177–178
Ricci, Christina, 79
Rickman, Alan, 108
Ritter, Thelma, 126, 214
Robb, AnnaSophia, 179–180
Robbins, Brian, 181–182
Robbins, Jerome, 143
Robbins, Tim, 151
Roberts, Julia, 160
Rocky, 185–186
Rodriguez, Robert, 183–184
Roman Holiday, 51, 52
Romano, Ray, 185–186
Romeo and Juliet (1968), 228
Rooney, Mickey, 243
Rose, Reginald, 62, 172
Rosemary's Baby, 163–164
Ross, Herb, 160
Ross, Katherine, 203
Rossellini, Isabella, 227
Rowlands, Gena, 187
Roxburgh, Richard, 86
Royal Tenenbaums, The, 25
Ruehl, Mercedes, 103, 230
Rule, Janice, 241
Rushmore, 84
Russell, Gail, 115
Russell, Kurt, 104, 188
Rydell, Bobby, 140

Sabrina, 51, 52
Sabu, 155
Saint, Eva Marie, 36, 52, 62
Sandler, Adam, 189, 233
Sarsgaard, Peter, 190–191
Saturday Night Fever, 167
Say Anything..., 38, 96
Scarface (1932), 196, 197
Scarface (1983), 30
Scheider, Roy, 24
Schneider, Maria, 90
Schoedsack, Ernest B., 111
Schreiber, Liev, 192–193
Schultz, Michael, 7

Schumacher, Joel, 194–195
Schwartzman, Jason, 84
Scofield, Paul, 50
Scorsese, Martin, 8, 23, 39, 50, 51, 130, 173, 177, 196–198, 222
Scott, George C., 124, 231
Searching for Bobby Fischer, 112, 113
Sellers, Peter, 32, 112, 175, 192, 208, 231
Sense and Sensibility, 108
Serre, Henri, 82
Seven Samurai, The, 3, 147, 201
Sharif, Omar, 34, 171
Shaw, Robert, 75, 99, 100
Shawshank Redemption, The, 150, 151
Shepard, Sam, 160
Shepherd, Cybill, 23, 174, 222
Sheridan, Ann, 223
Sheridan, Jim, 199–200
Shining, The, 106
Shire, Talia, 46, 84, 134, 185
Shoot the Piano Player, 53–54
Silence of the Lambs, The, 140
Sinatra, Frank, 164
Singin' in the Rain, 148
Singleton, John, 201–202
Sizemore, Tom, 184
Skerritt, Tom, 160
Skye, Ione, 38, 96
Smith, Jada Pinkett, 30
Something Wild, 74–76
Sorkin, Aaron, 66
Sound of Music, The, 15–16, 153
Spacek, Sissy, 241
Spacey, Kevin, 183
Spielberg, Steven, 75, 76, 199, 225
Splash, 6
Splendor in the Grass, 169, 236–237
Stallone, Sylvester, 185–186
Stanton, Harry Dean, 97
Stapleton, Maureen, 140
Star Wars, 136
Star Wars: Episode V—The Empire Strikes Back, 235
Starship Troopers, 15, 16
Staunton, Imelda, 203

Steel Magnolias, 160
Steiger, Rod, 36, 52, 62
Stevenson, Robert, 28
Stewart, James, 57, 94, 121, 238
Stiller, Ben, 25, 119
Sting, The, 99, 100
Stone, Oliver, 30
Straight, Beatrice, 26
Strasberg, Lee, 46, 134
Streep, Meryl, 1, 2, 116, 214
Sturges, John, 147
Sugar Cane Alley, 138, 139
Sutherland, Donald, 204–205
Swinton, Tilda, 206–207
Sykes, Wanda, 208–209

Talk to Her, 1
Tamiroff, Akim, 14
Taps, 123, 124
Tate, Larenz, 210–211
Taxi Driver, 23, 50, 173, 174, 222
Tender Mercies, 51, 220, 221
Terms of Endearment, 9–10, 116–117, 132–133
Theron, Charlize, 212–213
They Made Me a Criminal, 222–223
Thomas, Henry, 199
Thompson, Emma, 108
3 Women, 241
Thurman, Uma, 214–215
Time Bandits, 224–225
Time of the Gypsies, 192
To Each His Own, 127
To Kill a Mockingbird, 150, 151
To Sir, with Love, 218, 219
Todd, Beverly, 230
Tolkein, J. R. R., 180
Tombstone, 104
Tootsie, 68
Touch of Evil, 13–14
Tourneur, Jacques, 113, 142
Towne, Robert, 70, 216–217
Tracy, Spencer, 126
Trading Places, 181, 182
Travers, Henry, 94
Travolta, John, 167

Truffaut, François, 53, 82
Trumbo, Dalton, 52
Tucker, Chris, 81
Turman, Glynn, 7
12 Angry Men, 61, 62, 172
2001: A Space Odyssey, 21–22
Tyler, Liv, 179

Ullmann, Liv, 4
Underwood, Blair, 218–219
Uptown Saturday Night, 210

Van Dyke, Dick, 140, 154
Van Runkle, Theodora, 46, 134
Vaughn, Vince, 220–221
Vega, Isela, 115
Venora, Diane, 184
Verhoeven, Paul, 16
Viva Zapata, 61
Voight, Jon, 184
von Sydow, Max, 219

Wager, Anthony, 194
Wahlberg, Mark, 222–223
Walken, Christopher, 1
Walker, Joyce, 227
Walker, Paul, 224–225
Warden, Jack, 62, 172
Washington, Denzel, 226–227
Watanabe, Ken, 228
Watson, Emily, 233
Wayans, Keenan Ivory, 30
Wayne, John, 114, 115
Weaver, Dennis, 14
Welles, Orson, 13, 14, 66, 186
Wellman, William A., 147, 197
Werner, Oskar, 82
West Side Story, 143
What Ever Happened to Baby Jane?, 107
Wheel of Time, 190–191
Whitaker, Forest, 229–230
White Diamond, The, 190
Whiting, Leonard, 228
Wilder, Billy, 44, 57, 58
Wilder, Gene, 101, 152

Williams, John, 76
Williams, Olivia, 84
Williams, Robin, 6, 103, 177, 178
Willis, Bruce, 231–232
Willy Wonka & the Chocolate Factory,
    101–102, 152
Wilson, Flip, 210
Wilson, Luke, 25
Wilson, Owen, 25, 233–234
Wilson, Patrick, 235
Wilson, Rita, 79
Winger, Debra, 9, 10, 116, 132
Winslet, Kate, 106, 108
Wise, Robert, 16, 143
Witherspoon, Reese, 236–237
Wizard of Oz, The, 55, 129, 189
Woman of the Year, 125, 126
Wood, Elijah, 238
Wood, Evan Rachel, 239–240

Wood, Natalie, 143, 169, 236–237
Wood, Peggy, 16
Woodard, Alfre, 241–242
Woodward, Edward, 138, 139
Wray, Fay, 111
Wright, Teresa, 146
Wuthering Heights (1939),
    125–126
Wyler, William, 125

York, Michael, 156
Young, Burt, 185
Young, Gig, 115

Z, 88–89
Zallian, Steven, 113
Zeffirelli, Franco, 228
Zeta-Jones, Catherine, 243–244
Zhang Yimou, 230